First published 2006
Copyright © 2006 Thought Leaders Limited

National Library of Australia
Cataloguing-in-Publication data:

Ideas : original perspectives on life and business
from leading thinkers.

ISBN 0-9775724-0-4.

1. Business. 2. Life. I. Church, Matt.
(Series : Thought leaders ; 1).

658

Published by Thought Leaders Limited
PO Box 140, Seaforth NSW 2092 Australia
www.thoughtleaders.com.au

Editing by Ink Communications
(simone@inkcommunications.com.au)

Cover design and layout by Scope Design Group
(www.scopedesign.com.au)

Printed in Australia by Green and Gold Printing
(www.greenandgold.com.au)

Printed on sumo matt (cover) and nordset (text) by
Raleigh Papers (www.raleighpaper.com.au)

Disclaimer
The material in this publication is of the nature of general
comment only and does not represent professional
advice. It is not intended to provide specific guidance for
particular circumstances and it should not be relied on as
the basis for any decision to take action or not take action
on any matter which it covers. Readers should obtain
professional advice where appropriate, before making any
such decision. To the maximum extent permitted by the
law, the contributors, authors and publishers disclaim all
responsibility and liability to any person, arising directly
or indirectly from any person taking or not taking action
based upon the information in this publication.

"A mind, once stretched by a new idea, never regains its original dimensions."

OLIVER WENDELL HOLMES

A number of years ago I decided that the best job in the world would be to hang out with smart people and enjoy the results of better thinking and better conversations. Since then, it has been my privilege to sit alongside some brilliant thinkers as they 'unpack' quality ideas that can change the world.

The information age has passed and we are now entering the age of 'concept'. The ability to access information or data alone is no longer a premium – we don't need more experts to give us more information. What we need are people who can capture, package and deliver information in a way that goes beyond just bits and bytes. What we need are Thought Leaders.

In this book you will find 23 concepts from as many experts. The topics are as diverse as the people who present them, and this book itself is an example of the power of well-organised thought.

Each section follows a structured approach. Every idea is separated into three distinct elements, creating a consistent framework that gives form to intangible thoughts. Each concept is presented articulately in a declarative statement, then it is shown contextually in the form of a model or diagram, and finally, the concept is described in detail – or in other words – each of our Thought Leaders provides the 'stuff' that makes the point and paints the picture.

The methodology is unique to the Thought Leaders™ process and central to the Expert Development Programs that we run.

There is something exponential in the power of sharing ideas: I say something, and you grow that idea as a result of your thinking. This book is simply an explosion of ideas. The real power lies in what you think next.

When harnessed, the power of your mind is beautiful. You have read thousands of ideas already throughout your lifetime and you have had many thousands more – but ideas, if not shared, wither and die. If you wish to expand and learn how to share your thinking, visit www.thoughtleaders.com.au and download our special report on Thought Leadership.

Good thinking

Matt

MATT CHURCH
CEO

"Leadership is about your actions and reactions; about making decisions without deliberation; and about acting with confidence, but without recklessness."

Teamwork is about achieving something that would be impossible for an individual; and to build an effective team you need a leader. The greater the challenge facing the team, the greater the leader that is required. Based on my experience working within crisis and disaster situations with great leaders, I've learnt that whether we are in a position of leadership over many, a few, or the single most important person – ourselves – leadership matters.

leadership matters
PETER BAINES

EXIT
get out of it

FRANTIC
get into it

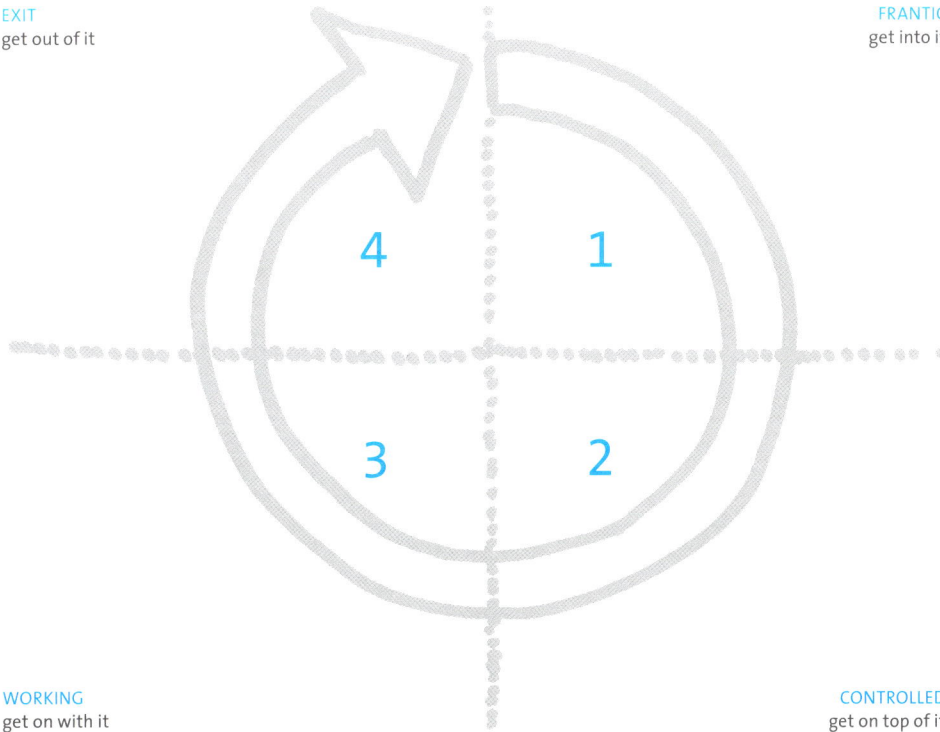

4

1

3

2

WORKING
get on with it

CONTROLLED
get on top of it

I've spent my career responding to crises. Many of us think that we deal with crisis on a daily basis through the general pressures and turmoil of our lives, and that's a fair call. But over the last few years I have dealt with situations that have brought a new perspective to what I used to call 'crisis'. You see, when I arrived at Wat Yan Yao in Thailand following the Boxing Day tsunami, and saw a couple of thousand bodies lying in the grounds of a temple, my view of what could rightfully be called a 'crisis' changed.

Responding to horrific scenes such as this is challenging enough, but what makes them a real crisis is that you are starting well behind the eight ball. When we arrived in Thailand there were 400 international specialists from 36 countries, and there was no appointed leader. There was no infrastructure to support these people; the resort area where we needed to work had been destroyed and was not fit to support the locals, let alone the influx of police and other specialists.

Working in crisis, there are a number of things that we need to be able to achieve in order to function effectively:

- we need to have clarity of purpose
- we need to be able to communicate (even when no one is speaking the same language)
- we need to build exceptional teams – fast
- and the overriding essential element that we need is strength and courage in leadership.

The true leaders in times of crisis are not mere figureheads, and often they are leaders without authority; they are leaders simply because they lead and others follow. So what makes a true leader? A true leader can make decisions without deliberation, they act with confidence but without recklessness, and they can turn chaos into calm. It is their actions and reactions that set them apart and cause people to want to follow them.

> When I arrived at Wat Yan Yao in Thailand following the Boxing Day tsunami, and saw a couple of thousand bodies lying in the grounds of a temple, my view of what could rightfully be called a 'crisis' changed.

Whether a leader is appointed or chosen, whether they are the leader of themselves or of a team of hundreds, they must know how to achieve results by harnessing the power of the resources available to them. Key to this in any crisis situation – whether it is an impending project deadline or a natural disaster – is understanding and being able to manage people through the stages of a crisis. Dealing with, and being part of any crisis is an incredibly emotional journey that invariably follows a cycle. Whether it's a crisis that will be over within an hour, or something like the response in Thailand that saw the international forensic community committed for twelve months, the emotional cycle is always the same – the only difference is the speed at which you and your team move through each of the four stages. Being able to recognise the stage of the crisis clock that the project, you or your team are at helps leaders to make the decisions and to implement the management strategies required to lead their team through the situation and beyond.

THE CRISIS CLOCK
The crisis clock is a tool to identify, manage and focus resources during a crisis. In my line of work, a crisis is an event such as a bombing or a tsunami – in yours it might be a product failure, a deadline, a HR issue or a strike action. I guarantee that you can position yourself somewhere on the crisis clock in relation to some aspect of your life today, whether it is in relation to your career, a project at work, the building of your home or a relationship crisis. It doesn't matter what it is, a crisis is a crisis, and this tool can help anyone dealing with a crisis to understand and manage what they need to do.

Each stage of the crisis clock presents its own challenges, from having people with too much energy to not having enough and wondering if they'll be able to pull out of it! There are three essential elements to being able to work through each stage and effectively deal with the crisis at hand. Let's look at each of the stages.

STAGE 1: FRANTIC – GET INTO IT

- **Look after yourself and your mates**
  - In crisis management we need to ensure that people are physically okay. There is a tendency for people to get caught up in the frantic energy and avoid sleep and food – someone has to look after the staff.
  - In a controlled response, where there is no 'crisis' element and there is time for planning, this is the stage when you consider the skill sets required to undertake the project.

- **Assess the boundaries – scope the project, but don't take too long**
  - When we first arrive at any type of crime scene, whether it's something of the scale of the Bali bombings or a single homicide, the first thing we assess is the size of the scene and the response required.
  - This is the point in time when you clearly define what the team will consider – that is, what is in and outside the scope of the project or response.

- **Deploy your resources – but stay in touch**
  - You need to get started; you need to stop talking and start doing what you are there to do.
  - In the deployment of your resources there needs to be control and appropriate communication and reporting. The extent of this will depend on various factors, including the size of the project, implications to the organisation and the likely duration.

STAGE 2: CONTROLLED – GET ON TOP OF IT

- **Plan response and duration – how long is this going to take?**
  - This is the time when the frantic response has abated and there is an opportunity to prepare a more strategic approach.

- In Thailand, it was at this stage that we wrote detailed position descriptions to ensure that the skill set of staff deployed from throughout the world was in accordance with what was required. We were also able to forecast the anticipated duration of the deployment.

- **Process the scene – just do what you're there to do**
  - Operations now have structure to them and there becomes a confidence in the way work is being done. People are very clear around what they need to do, how to do it and of equal importance, why they are doing it.

- **Gainful employment for all – who's doing all the work?**
  - The initial reaction to any crisis is to tip a whole heap of resources into the situation. Usually, the first response is to send as many people as possible, believing that everyone will have a job to do. However, one of the most destructive elements for the management team is having people on hand to help but not having a role for them. Having people at the scene of a disaster or crisis without gainful employment is untidy for many reasons, the management team needs to release or redeploy these resources, quickly!

STAGE 3: WORKING – GET ON WITH IT

- **Manage the energy – they will get tired**
  - The tiredness can be emotional and/or physical. Once the excitement leaves a project the work still has to be done. No matter how big it starts, whether it's the worldwide coverage that comes with an event such as the Bali bombings, the tsunami, or even an extravagant project launch, the hype will go – but the work still has to be done. The management team needs to acknowledge and manage the onset of this energy shift.

- **Develop an exit strategy – prepare to leave it with them**
  - No matter how fast the crisis clock ticks, there will be a need to leave, the project will come to an end. Managing the exit needs to be planned and during this third stage is when that needs to occur. How the project is left can be more important than many of the achievements along the way.

- **Report to stakeholders – let them know what is going on**
- Reporting and communicating is something that will be ongoing throughout each of the four stages, however, there is always a need to justify what has and has not occurred. The decisions made during a response to crisis are often reflected upon and judged at a later point in time by those in more comfortable environments.
- During the judgment of the response to a disaster there is a need for those who were in control, the decision makers, to justify their reasoning. The justification of actions will cover issues such as the deployment of staff, deviations from accepted principles and a detailed analysis of costs incurred. For the commander or project manager to be able to safely navigate their way through any inquiry they need to have made comprehensive notes that support their decision-making process. Anecdotal, or evidence from one's memory seldom suffices!

STAGE 4: EXIT – GET OUT OF THERE

- **Implement exit strategy – leave it with them**
- There comes a time when you go home and it is all left to someone else. How you leave it with them needs to be planned and how you leave requires equal planning. Working in disaster and crisis areas results in a significant emotional investment by the teams. Try as you might to remain emotionally detached from what is going on, it is just not possible. The fact that the team has been exposed to something significant needs to be acknowledged and then they need to be supported through that journey.

- **Handover – pass the baton**
- To ensure a smooth transition between teams, a timely and prepared handover needs to occur. The thing to remember when preparing the handover is that nothing is too simple to be included. When you first arrive, absolutely everything is new and challenging, after a while though it seems obvious, but remember that it wasn't obvious when you commenced your deployment.

- **Debrief and acknowledgement – sit back and reflect**
- There has to be a time to acknowledge what was done well, what can be done differently and what was learnt for next time.

Crisis is just the critical testing ground for leadership capabilities.

What I have learnt through my experience of building and leading Australian and international teams in times of crisis is that it is not about the crisis, it is not about being appointed to a certain position and it is certainly not about ego – it is about leadership. Crisis is just the critical testing ground for leadership capabilities.

I often reflect on what was achieved in responding to the crisis in Thailand. We had 400 forensic experts from around the world descend on a devastated area. There was no leadership in place, there was no time to prepare the response, the infrastructure was non-existent, and yet within a matter of days a process was put into place and an organisation built whose operations would equal that of any large company with many years' trading behind it. If there was one single factor that enabled all this to occur it was the strength of the leadership. Those who took responsibility for achieving the outcome, which in this case was to identify the 5,395 victims and send them home to their grieving loved ones, understood that *Leadership Matters.*

"After years of running my own small business and reading a truckload of business books, I realised that I was playing a game that I had little control over."

Have you ever played a game without the rulebook? Have you ever suspected that everyone else was playing a different game to you? A few years ago that was exactly how I felt. Just having that hunch, acknowledging that I might be onto something, and then investigating it was the turning point in my life. It seemed to me that there was a world out there where some people knew the rules to a 'secret' game that could compound their winnings and help them make a fortune for themselves, while the rest of us plodded along struggling to pay debt, save for retirement and escape the rat-race.

the essence of the deal
LIS BRANDSON

THE COMPONENTS OF DEAL MAKING

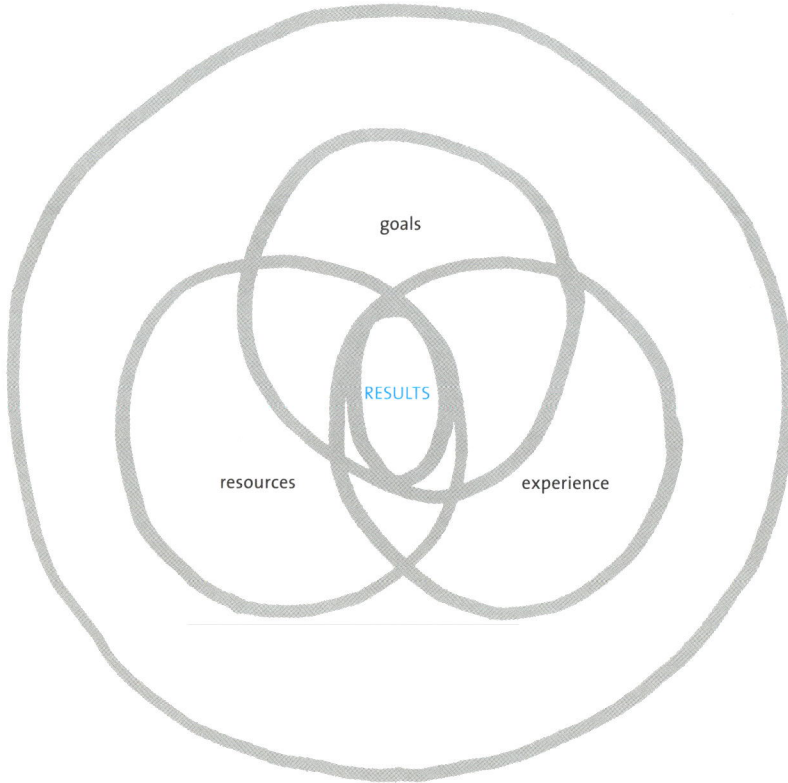

LIFE, IT HAS BEEN SAID, IS VERY MUCH LIKE A GAME

The first thing I discovered was that there are many games being played, all with different rules. I realised that every day everyone is participating in games, some consciously, but most unconsciously, and generally without knowing the rules.

What I noticed when I read the biographies of successful people and talked to local entrepreneurs was that they all shared an intuitive understanding of their field. They knew their industry intimately, they had uncovered the rules that could be bent, those that could be broken and the few that were sacrosanct, and then set about using that knowledge to their advantage. And it mattered little what industry they were in: retail sales, real estate, property development, share trading, direct sales, IT. I could find massive success stories in every one of these sectors as well as countless failures.

TO WIN, YOU NEED TO PLAY CONSCIOUSLY

That study left me with one core lesson – pick a game and learn its rules back-to-front, inside out and upside down.

I started to take my past experience in elite sport and dance and apply it to business. I remember one dance summer school when an international choreographer had us rapidly drill and learn a contemporary dance routine so well that we could instantly transpose the routine to perform it backward or starting on our other leg. That intimate understanding of the underlying rules and flow of a game – whether it is a recreational game, a relationship or a business is the key to unlocking the 'secret' world of success.

I decided to test my theory out on property development, with startling results. By simply applying the rules I was taught by master investors, I turned a kitty of $14,000 into a million dollar property portfolio within 12 months. Now, I'm not here to tell you the specific rules behind the game of real estate investing, but what I hope to do is inspire you to understand the importance of due diligence, modelling and never setting foot in a game until you know its underlying unbreakable rules.

Every one of us has experience with games and deals. We all learnt about deals when we were children through the games we played, through the games we watched others play, and most importantly, through the games we lost. If you don't know the 'no travel' rule of netball, you're going to lose the ball. If you don't know that in boxing the number one rule is 'protect yourself' you're going to get knocked out before you throw your first punch. And if you don't know to always protect your downside in real estate investing, and that you make your profit when you buy not when you sell, you'll become another victim of the property cycle.

> Understanding the underlying rules and flow of a game – whether it is a recreational game, a relationship or a business is the key to unlocking the 'secret' world of success.

THE GOAL

It is essential that you understand the goal of the game and check that it is in alignment with your own values and goals. I always ask myself these three questions:

1. What is the overt goal of the game?
2. What are the hidden agendas?
3. Is the prize worth the price?

While the overt goal – the upside – may be clearly defined, the covert goals may be more difficult to see in advance. The dealmaker may have the hidden goal of losing, the game may be a stalking-horse, or it could be a scam. Hidden goal agendas usually include the following:
• the need to be right / must be right
• the need to be loved / must be loved
• the need to win / must win.

It is important that you try to flesh out your own motivations and the motivations of the other players or the game could turn pear-shaped before you can identify what is going on and how to remedy the situation.

THE RESOURCES

Resources include everything you bring to the table, plus everything each of the players brings to the table, compared with your opponent's resources (if there is one). It determines your ability to stay in the game. Resources may include:

- **Access to credit:** This may determine the ultimate outcome because credit terms may ensure one player can outlast all other players.
- **Capacity to contribute:** In some games your own physical, mental or emotional resources may influence the result.
- **Your network of relationships:** In deals, your circle of influence is of key importance.

THE EXPERIENCE

Your experience will determine the relevance of particular games to your situation. I would always choose to play a game where I have experience that can be brought to the table. In a deal, experience is worth as much as the outcome and the resources.

Experience is not just the good stuff. What baggage and belief systems do you and the other participants bring to the table? How many games have you played consciously, how many have you won, lost or drawn? All of these factors will influence how well you play the game.

THE RESULTS

The outcome and what it means to you is the sum of your goals, resources and experiences. One way you can optimise your results is to play as a team. That is where a number of players come together to assist each other to get the result more easily. An investment consortium is an example of this. So is a company where the directors are participants. I have found that playing as a team produces the greatest results. It allows a pooling of all resources and experience.

Among the things that can torpedo a team approach are unresolvable personality clashes, or competing individual goals. Team playing is also challenging for some people because of their learning or personality style. For example, if you have an authoritarian leadership style then it makes it harder to have equal partners in a deal. You'll tend to go it alone, tough it out and employ help, rather than ask for help. If you have a compliant style, you run the risk of going along with decisions that should be debated. If you have a self-actualising style then decision making within the team can take longer, but statistically will result in greater success for the team and the individuals within the team.

Sometimes, the financial result doesn't live up to expectations, however you or your team may learn so much that the experience leads to the desire to do other deals together. In my opinion consortia based on a compounding of knowledge, experience and the ability to play as a powerful team leads to the best possible results for all concerned.

A FINAL THOUGHT

The most important thing is to start being conscious of the deals you make, taking responsibility for your part in the outcome, and learning from the experience so you can get even better returns in the future.

I would encourage you to take your first step into the world of deals – find a good team to work with and do your homework. Have a few 'dummy' runs, but then get in there and start accumulating some experience. It's the only way to become a great dealmaker!

"Work harder on being memorable! A great positioning statement and self introduction needs to be well-designed and delivered with impact."

We are not what we do – but we do need to be able to answer the question, "What do you do?" in a way that makes us better known and creates more business. As a card-carrying introvert, I find the prospect of commercial networking about as attractive as having a root canal treatment. Still, I recognise that without customers, clients and attendees at my events, my business would dry up quicker than a well in the outback.

the power of positioning
MATT CHURCH

THE POWERFUL POSITIONING MATRIX

FOCUS			
	you	it	them
high	obsession	uniqueness	purpose
medium	category	analogy	problems
low	history	examples	solutions

ENERGY

SO, WHAT TO DO?

For me, the pain was such that I searched for a way to take the effort out of the introduction process, and what I came up with was a practical model for creating powerful introductions. This nine-step positioning process achieves two things: first, it enables you to consistently answer the question, "What do you do?" with an appropriate level of detail. And second, it enables you to create a flexible positioning statement that can be creatively applied to any introduction situation.

CONSISTENT FLEXIBILITY!

It's been said that we all need a good 'elevator statement', a succinct 30-second sales pitch or service positioner that creates awareness about what we do and how it is unique or valuable. And while I don't remember a time when I successfully did business in an elevator, I do agree that we all need a way to answer the question, "What do you do?" so that we are positioned at the 'top of mind' should our customer ever face a situation where they need our products or services.

To approach the way we answer this question with a level of creativity, intelligence and purpose that is sadly lacking in most introductions, we need to think about the following:

The Focus Levels

As I started to explore the way people introduced themselves, I noticed patterns emerging. The first pattern that became clear was the focus of the introduction. The three options for focus are: to focus on YOU, to focus on IT, or to focus on THEM.

- YOU is obviously all about you, who you are, what you have done, and what you are into.
- IT is all about the activity, examples of how it has worked for someone, what it is like and maybe a few good stories about what it is that you do.
- THEM is all about the outcomes that your customers and clients achieve. You may ask questions, identify the key challenges they face or even get into solutions.

We are not what we do – but we do need to be able to answer the question, "What do you do?" in a way that makes us better known and creates more business.

When to use which?

While there are no hard and fast rules, I find that the more intimate the situation the more appropriate it is to answer the question with a focus on YOU. When you're unsure of whether you are in front of a prospect or not, you may focus on the activity that you perform, the IT. If the person you are speaking to is a clear prospect, then you would focus on the outcome, the THEM.

Here are some examples of how you might change the focus based on the environment:

SITUATION	FOCUS	
Dinner party	Personal	YOU
Networking event	Activity	IT
Prospect's boardroom	Outcomes	THEM

Of course, it may work to your advantage to juxtapose the focus – when you are versed in the nine positioning channels you can pick and choose your way around the grid as the situation dictates.

The Energy Levels

The second pattern that emerges in introduction situations is the energetic intensity of the introduction. There are three energy levels: LOW, MEDIUM and HIGH. Certain situations lend themselves to a more energetic and passionate introduction than others. Of course, some would argue that the higher the energy, the greater the impact on the other person – I don't agree. Take the person sitting next to you on an eight-hour flight; I don't know about you but I don't want a 'keen bean networking superstar' in seat 24a wowing me with her high-energy elevator statement. In this situation, a LOW energy introduction that grows in intensity as my interest grows may be more effective.

THE NINE INTRODUCTIONS
Let's talk about you

History – Low Energy

This is kind of like a verbal résumé outlining where you have been and what you have done. Be sure to edit out the irrelevant stuff. We learn to write résumés when we are young and before we've done anything. As a result we tend to pad them out, making as much as possible out of little. Now that you are a little older you can drop the stuff that you did years ago, or at least just sketch out the details. Only say that which is useful.

"I grew up in Newcastle, moved to Sydney to study, graduated in the late eighties and went to work in a prison. I then worked for the Australian Council for Health and Lend Lease, wrote a few books and ended up here on the corporate speaking circuit."

Category – Medium Energy

This channel is intentionally lacking in creativity. This is a black-and-white answer to the question. I often use this one as a trial balloon to see how interested the person asking the question is. You would answer with a professional category.

"I am a chartered accountant in a boutique firm with six partners."

"I am the senior tax partner for a multinational professional services firm."

"I am a strategic communications consultant."

"I run the IT department for a major bank."

Obsession – High Energy

Here you get to talk about your passion. This is the time to get fired up and rant a little about what it is you believe.

"I know that CEOs should spend less time preparing speeches and more time running businesses. Too many great leaders fail to think before they speak. If they simply got their ideas down more effectively they would make a greater impact when they spoke."

Now, let's talk about the activity

Examples – Low Energy

Choose an appropriate client case study, an example of someone you have been working with lately. The risk with this of course is that you choose an example that bears absolutely no relevance to the person in front of you, or one that may jeopardise your chances of working with their organisation. For example, if you were selling to a particular bank it may not help your case to discuss the work you have done for a competitor.

"One client we worked with recently had a problem getting their internal sales team to move from a product-based selling process into a relationship-based environment. Over six months we moved the incentive schemes and culture from having a focus on transactions to having a focus on relationships. They noticed a 40 per cent positive shift in client retention, and this looks like impacting the profit positively by another $250,000 this quarter alone."

Analogy – Medium Energy

This channel is particularly useful if you sell an intangible service or a new category of product or service. You draw a comparison between an already established concept and what you do.

"We are like a sports management company for information experts."

Uniqueness – High Energy

Here, you try to set yourself apart from others in your field. This is where you get to state your unique selling proposition and make a distinction between yourself and others. Whatever the masses are doing, try to position some part of what you do as contrary or opposed to this.

"While I am a lawyer, I am also a chartered accountant. This means we can handle all parts of the deal for you. We find this saves our clients time and money."

Finally, let's talk about the outcome

Solutions – Low Energy

This is similar to a case study or example, but here you actually state the benefits you create for others. It's often easy to ask a question that explains why you have created a certain solution.

"Do you find that you are spending too much time stuck in the day-to-day running of your business? We have created a personal effectiveness system that allows most people to get more done in less time. Our average client finds an extra three days' productivity per month when using our system."

Problems – Medium Energy

A problem is best described as the day-to-day internal dialogue your target has around what they do. When you start speaking about what's on their mind they truly engage with your products and services.

"The biggest problems in any law firm are keeping good staff, and moving from a fee-for-service model to a value-based advice model. Our business addresses these problems and creates a future-proof environment for any mid-sized law firm to grow."

Purpose – High Energy

This is where you express the client's reason for being in a way that shows you are aligned. You express how what you do is a perfect fit for their purpose.

"Here at 'Cocktail Capers' we realise that you should have as much fun at your own party as you would at someone else's. That's why we take care of everything from start to finish. You get to feel like you can just go to sleep at the end of the evening and know that when you wake up the next morning it's as if the party was held somewhere else."

A FINAL WORD ON FLEXIBILITY

There's no doubt that there are more ways that we could introduce ourselves, these nine channels are simply a starter's guide. I do know that I can only remember three things, so by working in each of the three focus levels I can easily recall the three energy choices. And if you're short on time, just use the three mid-level approaches for a use-anywhere introduction: Category + Analogy + Problems.

SOME WORKED UP EXAMPLES

Each of these examples demonstrate the use of all nine of the introduction techniques.

FIRST STEP COMMUNICATIONS (WEB DESIGN BUSINESS)

(History)	"I have a computer science degree."
(Category)	"I'm a web designer."
(Obsession)	"I love creating websites that make money, rather than cost money."
(Example)	"One client invested $5,000 with us and made over $100,000."
(Analogy)	"Think of us as a hardware store rather than a carpenter – we give you the tools and the guidance, and you create the products."
(Uniqueness)	"That's what makes us different. In fact, we don't even do web 'design', because the design will change over time for your business."
(Solutions)	"We solve that by giving you simple tools to update your site yourself."
(Problem)	"You see, that's a problem that many businesses have – their business changes but their website stays the same. And it's too expensive and too difficult to change your site yourself."
(Purpose)	"Because, after all, your business is not about web design; it's about…"

THOUGHT LEADERS LIMITED (MANAGEMENT COMPANY)

(History)	"Our team have all published books, run speaking businesses or been coaches."
(Category)	"We all came together to create a management company."
(Obsession)	"We are obsessed with leveraging expertise and helping clever people to become commercially smart about what they do."
(Example)	"One of our clients increased their billings from $180,000 per annum to more than $1.2 million in under 36 months."
(Analogy)	"We operate like a sports management company for clever people."
(Uniqueness)	"I guess the fact that we have all been there and done what our clients wish to achieve is what makes us stand out."
(Solutions)	"We help experts capture, package and deliver what they know so that they can make more money from it."
(Problems)	"Most people undervalue what they know and are so close to their expertise that they don't have the clarity to see what other ways they can leverage what they know."
(Purpose)	"The point is that we want people who know a lot to be recognised and valued for what they provide."

"Great experiences. We all want them; we crave them. They drive the way we live."

As customers today we are spoilt for choice. In a crowded marketplace, the key differentiator driving our buying decisions is the overall experience we have, not merely the choice of the product or service. It's why we will drive past any number of businesses that could meet our needs, to find the one that treats us the way we prefer. More than ever, we are consciously seeking out positive experiences – experiences that make us feel good.

how to create unbreakable customer relationships
IVEN FRANGI

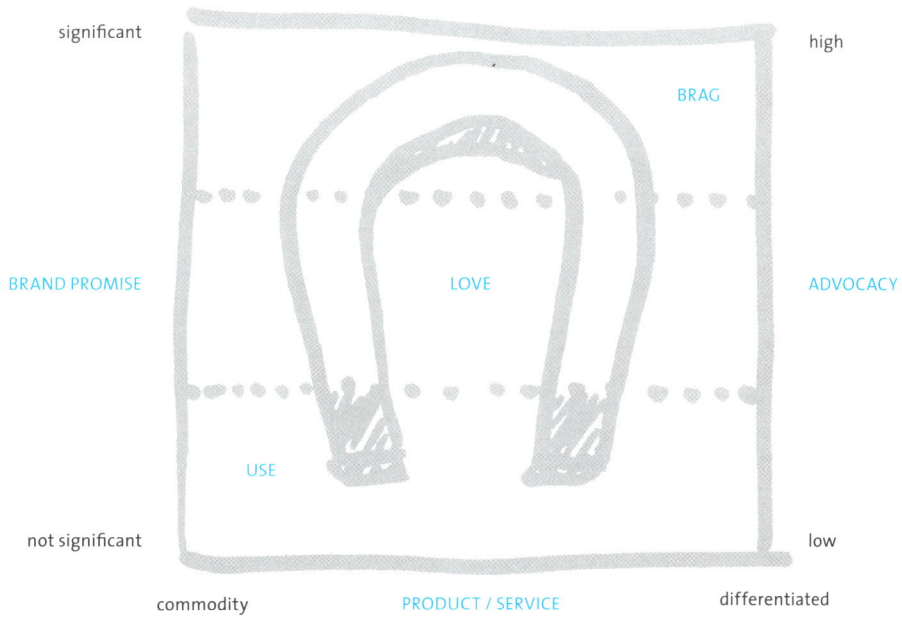

significant

high

BRAG

BRAND PROMISE

LOVE

ADVOCACY

USE

not significant

low

commodity

PRODUCT / SERVICE

differentiated

According to a *Beyond Philosophy* UK survey, '71 per cent of business leaders say that CEM is the next competitive battleground'. And, '44 per cent of customers say that their customer experiences are bland or negative'. *BusinessWeek* (19 December, 2005) called CEM '…one of the ideas that could shape your future'.

Magnetic Xperiences are not an accident and don't happen by chance – they are planned, predictable and profitable.

The businesses that create unbreakable customer relationships and transform their customers into advocates understand that every time they do business, their customers have an experience – either good or bad. And they work hard to ensure that the experience they deliver is one that customers will value and come back for, again and again.

Until recently, Customer Relationship Management (CRM) and customer service have been the predominant tools in the kit of strategies to grow customer revenue. Others include customer loyalty, customer satisfaction, marketing and most recently, branding. Each has delivered varying degrees of effectiveness. Customer Experience Management (CEM) is the next business imperative. It provides the framework and architecture that leverages all of these tools to create an experience that attracts and retains customers. I work with my clients to migrate customers from being people who use their products to being advocates who brag about them. We do this by creating a Magnetic Customer Xperience. Magnetic Xperiences are not an accident and don't happen by chance – they are planned, predictable and profitable.

CUSTOMER EXPERIENCE IS THE NEXT BUSINESS IMPERATIVE BECAUSE:

- CRM hasn't delivered better customer relationships, just better information about customers.
- Customer satisfaction is no longer enough; satisfied customers may defect to a competitor.
- Customer loyalty that is based only on loyalty rewards programs has been difficult to sustain.
- Customers want their values reflected in the businesses with which they deal.
- Customers who are advocates create business value and drive growth.

THE BRAND IS THE EXPERIENCE – THE EXPERIENCE IS THE BRAND

Whether we realise it or not, we all want to be aligned with products, services and brands that make us feel better about ourselves and who we are. Then, we want to tell others about why they make us feel better, special, needed, recognised wanted or validated. That's not marketing; it's basic human nature.

Like everyone else, as a child I desperately wanted to go to Disneyland *(a highly differentiated offering – refer to model)*. The TV shows and merchandise told me it was the happiest place on Earth *(the brand promise was high on significance)*. Finally, at the age of 17, I arrived at the Anaheim California entrance with great expectations. That day was one I will never forget, full of fun, laughter and surprises. I used the product (the theme park) and I loved it *(the brand promise matched the actual experience)* and so I became an advocate. I remembered and *bragged* about that experience for years. The Disney brand promise is so strong that it can even be inherited! Many years later, in France, I made sure that my seven-year-old son also enjoyed that same Disney brand experience – and now he's an advocate and brags about it too.

The closer your brand promise is to what your customers actually value, the more successful you will be. Ikea, Starbucks, Apple, Southwest Airlines, Singapore Airlines, Harley Davidson, Dell, Nordstrom and others clearly define what experience they will deliver and they work hard to make that come true in every interaction and at every touch point. These companies have surpassed simple measures of satisfaction and loyalty, and created customers who are advocates – that is, people who willingly brag about their experience and why it was so outstanding. Any business can hang out a shingle and tell the marketplace it exists. But what these and other successful businesses do differently is follow the principles of the Magnetic Xperience model.

Amazon is another excellent example, it originally created a significant brand promise built around offering any book you want, from any author, delivered to you just about anywhere in the world. A *significant brand promise* can only be made when you understand what it is your customers value and how you will translate that value into your offer. Amazon recognised that the experience of going to a bookstore is one that people enjoy. Customers *value* being able to peruse the shelves, see the range of titles, read excerpts and compare one book with another. So they had to answer the question, why would customers choose to give up their in-store experience? To deliver a brand promise that was significant they had to innovate, they had to find a way to deliver customers a better than in-store experience online.

Amazon customers typically fall into the three phases outlined in the model before becoming advocates. Initially, they are apprehensive but they begin to use the service. Those who appreciate the innovation and the expanding range of services love the concept and convenience. Those who value having the world's largest range of books at their fingertips, which can be delivered to their door, become advocates. For them, the Amazon bookstore is highly differentiated from the one at the local mall. And as advocates they brag about Amazon to others.

Amazon's share of wallet (the percentage amount of a customer's total spend on a product or service in one business) is the industry leader. The online prompt *'other people who bought this book also bought'* has meant that the number of books per sale has surpassed the average sales in a bricks and mortar bookstore. Amazon is clearly differentiated, not only because it is virtual, but because it has turned virtual into real. The level of advocacy is what has driven it from a standing start less than ten years ago to (at the time of writing) thirty-four categories from furniture and homewares, to baby needs. The Amazon Xperience is clearly Magnetic!

BUILD A RELIABLE, ROBUST, REPEATABLE AND MAGNETIC CUSTOMER XPERIENCE...OR BUILD AN EXIT STRATEGY

Organisations like Amazon know that making the strategic shift to delivering Magnetic Customer Xperiences is about moving the focus from the internal business processes and the way customers are managed, to better understanding the customer's perspective, how they interact with the organisation and how those interactions can be engineered to deliver an outstanding experience – every time. Measuring how many advocates a business has is the best yardstick for establishing the level and consistency of the customer experience. New technology enables this measurement to be done more easily.

There is a predictable process that we all go through as consumers to choose what we want, and from whom.

1. **Scan.** We constantly have our radar on for what we may want.
2. **Match.** When we find something, we match it to our criteria.
3. **Decide.** If it matches our criteria we decide to acquire it or not.
4. **Commit.** After we decide, if we are able to, we acquire what we want.
5. **Use.** We experience using or owning our purchase.
6. **Love.** If it meets or surpasses our expectations, we love it.
7. **Brag.** If we are delighted, we become advocates.

At each stage of the process we have an experience. That experience may be positive or negative. It's the quality of the experience at each stage that will determine whether or not we move to the next. Some of the factors that may either make or break the experience include: availability, accuracy of information, quality, options, price, delivery, accessibility, location, the environment, and the product or service itself.

Like magnets, experiences have two poles: a 'positive' which attracts, and a 'negative' which repels. Think of every interaction your customers, or potential customers, have as being magnetic. Each interaction will either attract or repel them. In other words the experiences at each touch point will either make or break the opportunity to go to the next stage.

What creates advocates? Advocates for your business have moved past loyalty to another level. In order to gain customer loyalty, you need to engage not only a customer's mind, you need to engage their emotions. By doing something significant for a customer you create appreciation. If you can create experiences that are enjoyable, satisfying or rewarding then the emotions are in play.

To create advocates you must orchestrate the people, processes and technology in the business to focus on a shared goal. Then, for each touch point, you must establish the appropriate measure to evaluate progress.

THE KEY XPERIENCE QUESTIONS

There are some basic questions to ask that will establish the way forward. The first question is: what do our customers value or find significant about our products or services? As well as standard market research, a more useful result is obtained by watching what customers do and how they behave when interacting at the touch points. Observe the makers and breakers. This will give you clues. Once you have established the type or level of experience you want to deliver you have to evaluate each functional area (people, processes and technology) and decide what needs to be achieved.

• For each of the functional areas set goals for performance.
• Then, determine how you will measure the results.
• Next, set the benchmark to be achieved.
• Last, decide the financial impact of achievement.

For example: imagine you run a business that rents computer equipment with annual contracts. A *goal* is to renew existing customer contracts. A *measure* would be the customer renewal rate. The *target* would be a desired percentage, say, a 10 per cent increase on last year. The balance sheet impact would be monthly cash flow. By establishing a clear experience proposition and linking that to an outcome that can be tracked, the effectiveness of the delivered experience can be measured and managed.

A reliable, robust and Magnetic Customer Xperience delivers tangible results, among them:
• Maximising the wallet share for what you sell.
• Increasing the number of products you sell per customer.
• Increasing the acquisition of new customers.
• Minimising customer churn.
• Increasing the number of customers who are advocates for your business.

World-leading Magnetic Customer Xperiences are designed and constructed like a great building – nothing is left to chance. The design is intentional, consistent and clearly differentiates the business from its competitors.

> To create advocates you must orchestrate the people, processes and technology in the business to focus on a shared goal.

SEVEN ACTIONS TO CREATE UNBREAKABLE CUSTOMER RELATIONSHIPS

1. **Appreciate that you already have an experience-based business.** The question is whether the experience you are delivering is the one you've designed or just the one that is happening as a default. Everyone in your organisation and everything you do creates a customer experience. These are what Jan Carlson best described in the title of his best-selling book, *Moments of Truth.*

2. **Decide what your brand stands for and be different – for the right reasons.** The experiences you design will be related to what you want your brand to deliver. David Hall is 'The Clean Plumber' (www.thecleanplumber.com.au). His brand promise is significant, and differentiated; it taps into what many people who use plumbers find frustrating – the fact that many plumbers are less than reliable and leave a mess when they go. With brand clarity, David designed an experience and behaviour template so that his team can deliver on the brand promise every time. And he is cleaning up, with 400 per cent growth in the past three years.

3. **The experience drives everything – get everyone in your business on the same mission.** Woody (Woodruff) Driggs, managing partner of operational CRM at Accenture says, *"CEM starts by getting everyone who is important to the customer experience in a room. We are constantly amazed to discover how often this is the first time that the key people from marketing, advertising, sales and service have talked to one another about what the customer experience should be".* Experiences are built on three pillars: your people, your processes and your technology. Get everyone together – not just sales, marketing and service, but everyone in your organisation – and focus on understanding the current experience you deliver, what your customers' expectations are, and identifying the gaps between the two. The challenge is to match the delivery of your unique brand values with the most critical needs and expectations of your target customer.

4. **It's not about being five-star – it is about being consistent to your brand.** Ikea isn't luxurious. In fact, it can be difficult to get around with all the crowds and the 'one direction' store layout. There is little customer service, which you have to queue for. Then there are long queues to buy anything, and more queuing to pick it up. Then you go home and have to make it yourself. What an experience! Yet the founder of Ikea has become one of the richest men in the world. Half of my office furniture comes from Ikea. Customers know they can see everything on display, try things in the store, and take them back. Ikea has designed an experience that offers customers a great range, real choice and great value. The brand promise is significant, the products are differentiated – and repeat purchase behaviour is extremely high.

5. **Create experiences worth bragging about.**
It's easy to get excited about Amazon.com because it's a pleasure to use. And you easily find yourself buying additional items thanks to the recommendations they make based on their '*people who bought this book also bought these*' offers. After flying Singapore Airlines, people talk about the friendly staff and the gentle service. Ask an Apple user why they like their Mac and you will see evangelism. Speak to a Harley owner and their face lights up. Stories of

Nordstrom service are legendary. None of this is an accident. Disneyland didn't just happen. We all want great experiences and we are actually delighted to become advocates. Is the experience you deliver worth bragging about? Is it one that people will pay for?

6. **Choose technology and information platforms to suit your customer experience and business requirements, not the other way around.**
Technology is an important part of your 'people, processes and technology' triad. Having a system that can give you a single view of the customer and help to manage what you are learning about the customer is crucial. The challenge is to get the information platform to meet your needs – not the other way around. IT supports the enterprise. There are now systems that will track advocacy, the quality of the customer experience and manage the touch point interface across the entire business. Choosing the one that is best for your business is critical.

7. **Evaluate where you are now and what you need to do next.** Where is your business now on an experience basis? Is there a long or short way to go? Are you ready to consider building a Magnetic Customer Xperience? The easiest way to find out is by completing the Magnetic Customer Xperience Evaluation. You can do it yourself in just a few minutes. Go to www.cxm.com.au and click on the 'Magnetic Xperience Evaluation'. It's designed to give you a snapshot of where you are on the path to designing and delivering a significant, differentiated and advocate-creating customer experience.

> Give your customers an experience that they can't get anywhere else, and they won't go anywhere else.

Your business becomes magnetic when it moves from being product and service-centric to being truly customer experience-centric. Just like a magnet, customers will be drawn to your business. *

"Leaders, pull out your swords and use them for good. Your heart will carry you to a place far beyond what you can see today."

You are a leader. Whether you are a parent, a CEO, an architect, a priest, a waiter, a sister or a brother, you are a leader. A leader is someone who affects the people around them so that their experience of the world is better for knowing them. And remarkable leaders are people who have a remarkable purpose, vision and qualities, and act from that place. How can you become a remarkable leader and live your leadership to its fullest potential? By having the courage to stop – to stop going for goals at any cost, to stop being a victim of people and circumstances, and to stop pretending that you can't really change the world for the better.

becoming a remarkable leader
GISÈLE GAMBI

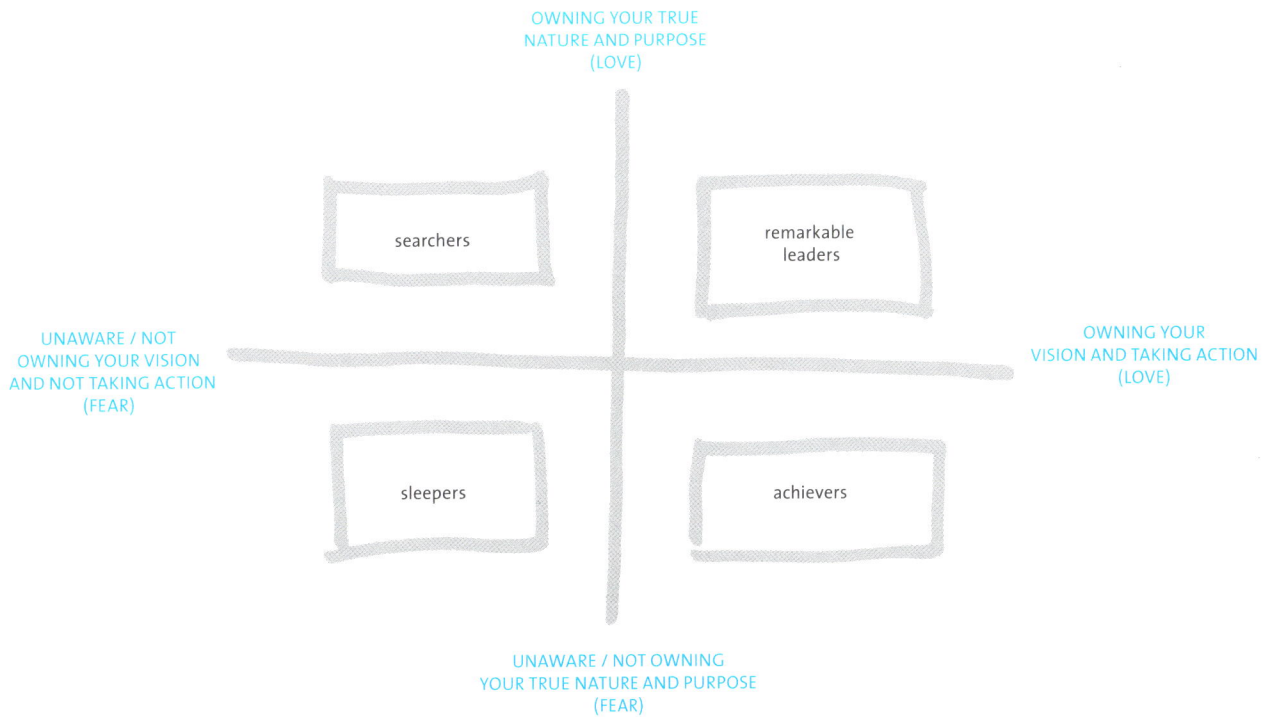

Remarkable leaders are real people who live their remarkable purpose, qualities and vision.

The first step a remarkable leader takes is to assume whole responsibility for the life they have created. They know that consciousness and self-awareness are the key ingredients to magnificent leadership.

A top range, high-performance car may look impressive, have all the latest trimmings and cost a lot of money, but if the engine doesn't perform it doesn't matter how good it looks, it won't get you from A to B and it won't meet your expectations. Similarly, as a leader you may be a Harvard graduate, work for the most prestigious company and wear the latest Italian suits, but if you don't have your 'engine' in working order, all of the other trimmings will be meaningless. So, let's begin by lifting the bonnet and looking at how your engine runs.

As human beings, living in this seemingly physical world, fear is at the core of most people's behaviour, both consciously and unconsciously. Fear that we won't be good enough, powerful enough, loved enough or safe enough; fear that there's not enough time, money or ability for us to do the things we'd love. When fear is the underlying driver of behaviour, competition, aggression, conflict, stress and illness result. When fear is the fuel, we may or may not achieve our goals – but even when we do it is never with ease, peace, joy and true fulfilment. When fear is the motivator, it is always focused internally on what we can do to keep ourselves powerful, admired, safe and secure.

Remarkable leaders dare to understand their fears so that they can recognise when they are operating this way, and make the conscious choice not to. While even the most self-confident leader still experiences fear at

times, they have an inner knowing that they are greater than what they fear and that they would be robbing others of their gifts if they were to succumb to it.

What are your fears? If you could play out your worst nightmare in your work or family life, what would that look like? Do you fear not being good enough? Are you unable to trust? Have you noticed how loud your 'chatter monkey', the voice of fear is? How often do you act on these voices and believe them to be true? Take a moment to answer these questions by jotting down whatever comes to mind. Then, close your eyes, take three deep breaths, and picture yourself on a stage acting out these fears. How do you behave when fear is the driver? What results do you get and what price do you pay? You may find yourself experiencing déjà vu – different situations and people, but with similar limited outcomes.

> Remarkable leaders know that their being in this world is not incidental, that it is about so much more than meeting budgets, deadlines or driving the kids to school.

Remarkable leaders display two other characteristics that allow them to live out their leadership potential.

First, they believe in their heart, soul or spirit. They know that it is extraordinary and that it contains all of the strengths, abilities and talents that are unique to them. They recognise that among all of the people in the world, their 'true nature' is unique to them. They may be compassionate, visionary, creative, courageous, able to create change or abundantly loving. This goes beyond how someone would usually describe themselves, and way beyond how a personality typing system would classify them. Your true nature holds no fear, malice or need to manipulate. The fuel behind your true nature is love.

Your heart also contains your purpose in life – what it is that you are here to do. Remarkable leaders know that their being in this world is not incidental, that it is about so much more than meeting budgets, deadlines or driving the kids to school. Love is the common denominator behind every person's life purpose – whether it is Oprah Winfrey raising people's awareness about confronting social issues, or Richard Branson inspiring people to think big and challenge the status quo. Remarkable leaders are courageous in owning their purpose wholeheartedly, and often take a leap of faith into the unknown. Of course they have fear about moving into their life's purpose, but they place that fear in the backseat and put their heart in the driver's seat.

Second, remarkable leaders don't simply own their true nature and purpose, they have a vision of it created from their heart and they take action to realise it. They grow their vision from a tiny seed, trusting that it will take shape. They are truthful about where they are in relation to achieving their ultimate goal, and take direct steps to bridge the gaps. As they see their vision come to fruition, the momentum they gain leads to even more action.

Sometimes remarkable leaders slip off the path due to the fear that they feel. But when they do, they are honest with themselves and they stop. They make a choice to not make decisions from this place, they reconnect to their vision and start taking direct and immediate action again.

Have you ever met your heart? Can you describe it? How would you define your true nature and the purpose that is unique to you? What about your vision? Is it created from your heart or from what you or others think you should do?

Why is it that there are so few remarkable leaders in the world? How many people do you know who have so much potential but fail to see or live it? We already know that fear is what inhibits leaders from truly stepping up and becoming remarkable, so let's look at this in more detail. As we have discussed, remarkable leaders:

- understand their fears
- know the power of their heart, and own their true nature and purpose
- have a vision and act on it.

But what happens when leaders are unconscious to this, when they have met their heart but fail to act on it, or when they act from fear?

Sleepers are people who are unaware of their potential and vision. They get by, living unconsciously, and are often the victim of people and circumstances. They believe that they have no choice in life and you'll often hear them say, "It wasn't meant to be," and, "There's nothing I can do about it".

Searchers are people who have tasted their true nature and purpose, but are constantly thinking that there must be more for them to know or have before they can live their potential. As they don't have a clear vision and they feel uncertain of their life path, they are always looking for the answer and therefore take little or no action. You'll often see them feeling confused, frustrated, in a state of inertia and at times, depressed.

True leadership means taking personal responsibility for being the best you can be.

Achievers are people who have a very strong vision and go for their goals at all costs. As they are unaware of their innate resources they achieve success through lots of hard work, which leaves them feeling exhausted. And because they expend so much energy achieving their vision, they don't have enough personal resources leftover to have everything in their life and they therefore compromise on family, health and other interests. You'll often see them either 100 per cent 'on' or 100 per cent 'off'. Many public leaders who get results through lots of effort are likely to be achievers.

Remarkable Leaders are people who know that they are living their fullest potential and have witnessed their own magnificence. They are on-purpose and feel the true fulfilment that comes from living a life filled with meaning. They have a vision created from their heart and take personal responsibility for realising it by being authentic and focused on what they want to achieve. Remarkable leaders lead from love and utilise synergy to create 'everybody wins' outcomes. There is little or no cost or compromise in the world of a remarkable leader as they know that anything is possible if they are committed and come from the heart.

Do you recognise any of these behaviours or leadership styles in yourself? Many people live in the realm of the Sleeper, Searcher and Achiever modes. For the most part, this is unconscious behaviour, and as such it is very powerful in inhibiting people from being who they really are. Here are a few prescriptions that will help you to step out of these limiting modes.

IF YOU ARE A SLEEPER:

- **Start asking yourself some questions.** Do you enjoy what you do? What do you enjoy? What don't you enjoy? How would you describe your style of leadership? How would others describe your style of leadership? Ask six people in your life to answer this (family, friends and colleagues).
- **Be conscious every day** and start to create some intentions about what you want and how you want to be.

IF YOU ARE A SEARCHER:

- **Choose goals** (one or two to start with) taken from your vision and decide to complete them.
- **Take action,** more action…and even more action.
- **Don't judge the outcome.** Just appreciate that you have left the starting blocks.

IF YOU ARE AN ACHIEVER:

- **Be honest with yourself** in relation to what you compromise on in your life and what it is costing you.
- **Stop.** It usually isn't a matter of life or death.
- **Connect with your innate skills and abilities** and consciously be that person every day. Achieve from this place and notice the difference.

True leadership means taking personal responsibility for being the best you can be. Imagine what the world would be like if more of us gave as much importance to our hearts as we do to our minds. Imagine a world full of remarkable leaders all working with other remarkable leaders and doing things from purpose and potential. When a combination of hearts and minds comes together, powerful synchronistic results are created beyond what you could ever imagine.

How would you like to affect the people around you so that their experience of the world is better for knowing you?

DISCOVERING YOUR HEART

This is an exercise that will enable you to connect with your heart, to see who you are in your fullest leadership potential and what your vision looks like. It will take approximately 30 minutes, and you may wish to complete it in an uninterrupted space, somewhere where you are able to switch off and simply 'be' – perhaps in the garden or in a quiet room listening to beautiful music. This exercise was created by a student of ours, Sarah Morgan, whose leadership is about facilitating people to live a life based on truth.

Sit comfortably and take three breaths, inhaling through your nose and exhaling through your mouth. On each exhalation, allow the weight of your body to drop down and allow any tension or tiredness to flow effortlessly away. Spend a few moments simply following the movement of your breath in and out of your body, watching your belly expand and contract, and your chest rise and fall. If thoughts come, gently let them go and come back to your breath.

Now bring your attention to your heart, the essence of your being, containing your most precious gems, your innermost beauty, your true nature and purpose. Sit with that for a moment.

Now imagine a life, your life, without limitation or fear, your life with infinite possibilities. Of what do you dream? Allow 10 minutes to imagine this and then capture what you receive on paper.

When you are complete, close your eyes and return to your heart space and breathe into it. Now move your attention deeper inside your heart, to the core of your being and from this place ask yourself, if I could be a remarkable leader in the world how would I be? How would I be in my true nature? What would my life purpose be? If I could do whatever I wanted to do, what would I be doing? Who would be in my life? Take 15 minutes to imagine this and then capture what you receive on paper. Accept and allow everything that comes up.

When you are complete, close your eyes and return to your heart space and breathe into it. Consider for a moment what you have written so far. Now tell me, what would you need to let go of or release to invite the possibility of having this in your life? Once you know, write this down and come back to full consciousness.

This is an excellent process to complete on a regular basis to better understand your unique gifts, talents and purpose. If you give yourself just 30 minutes each week to connect with your heart, you will be more aware of your true nature, purpose and vision and able to step into your own remarkable leadership. ❦

"Many people fail to live the lives they were meant to live; they may excel in business, but sacrifice their leadership, their personal life and themselves in the process."

Leveraging your life, leadership, business and community focuses on the powerful effect that high-impact mentoring, teaching and advising can have on individuals, leaders, businesses and communities. When someone is assisted to get great clarity on their purpose, and powerfully mentored in the proven experiential principles of the Life Journey, Leadership Journey and Business Journey, they will make an extraordinary 100x progress through the power of leverage.

leveraging your life, leadership, business and community
DR ADRIAN GEERING

100X MODEL / LEVERAGING YOUR LIFE, LEADERSHIP, BUSINESS AND COMMUNITY

SUSTAINED PERSONAL MENTORING,
DEVELOPMENT AND LEVERAGING

CLARITY OF PURPOSE

LIFE, LEADERSHIP AND BUSINESS DEVELOPMENT PROCESS

life
journey

leadership
journey

business
journey

community
journey

In working with leaders, CEOs and businesses around the world for the last 20 years, what has become clear is that the key message for the new millennium is to leverage your life, leadership and business. It is no longer enough for leaders of any organisation to just focus on their business and forget their leadership and life roles. To be a world-class person, an effective leader running a high-performing business, it is essential to be multidimensional and to tap into the infinite riches and untapped potential that exists within each one of us.

The world of business has changed dramatically in the last few years with: 9/11; rising oil prices; the constant threat of terror attacks; increasing global competition; severe staffing shortages; the looming Baby Boomer exodus from the workforce; the changing attitudes of Generations X and Y to work; multicultural conflict; increasing expectations throughout society; manipulation by powerful minority leaders; ineffectiveness in governments at all levels; and the rate of technological change. These massive changes create an environment of enormous stress and pressure.

Many current day leaders have failed to deal effectively with the prevailing issues facing them, including: constant pressure for immediate responses and results through being accessible 24/7 via email, mobile phones and texting; the pressure to perform in increasingly competitive marketplaces; the increasing costs of doing business through employing scarce labour; and increasing costs of raw materials and other business inputs. This all contributes to creating ongoing demands, greater pressure, increased uncertainty and unpredictability.

These three case studies illustrate the plight of many modern senior managers.

- Bill is a successful CEO of a growing international business with locations throughout the world. Inevitably, his work entails a lot of international travel, so much in fact that Bill has neglected his family, himself and his health.
- Jack is the managing partner of a growing professional services firm with branches interstate. He is always busy with meetings within the firm, with major clients, and regular weekly dinner events. Add to this his hectic interstate travel schedule and Jack finds himself exhausted, unfit and experiencing ongoing ill health.
- Phil is the CEO of a very successful business with locations around Australia and overseas. The industry that his company serves is experiencing serious restructuring and consolidation, and profitability has been reduced by 50 per cent. Phil has diversified the business and is ahead of the game but this has come with prolonged absences away from home and impacts on his relationships with those closest to him.

> To be a world-class person, an effective leader running a high-performing business, it is essential to be multidimensional and to tap into the infinite riches and untapped potential that exists within each one of us.

In each of these examples, some questions can be posed:
- How did these leaders contribute to their circumstances?
- What could they have done differently?
- Does being successful in business mean that you have to sacrifice your family, yourself and your wellbeing?
- What could each of these leaders do to leverage themselves?

The leadership and business models of the past are not greeted with enthusiasm by the emerging generations. They have indeed, to a great extent, served as a grim warning of what not to do and what to avoid: workaholism; broken relationships and marriages; absentee parents; unbalanced lives; unfulfilled dreams; living time-poor; the inability to be content and enjoy the present; and poor health caused by enormous stress.

Today's business leaders serve as a cautionary role model to the emerging generation who are no longer prepared to sacrifice their lives and their leadership potential for business achievement alone. The emerging generation wants to be self-directed, autonomous and fulfilled. They do not want to sacrifice who they are in order to follow in the footsteps of their parents or peers. The twenty-something son of a successful CEO recently told me that he has let his father know that he will not work seven days a week and sacrifice his family and his life. To him, being successful in all areas of his life is more important than business success alone.

The future of leadership is about making different choices. In the past, many people chose to be successful at the expense of their life, their health and their happiness. And in so doing they have significantly affected their own and their family's lives. Leaders have admitted that the most important person that has lost out is themselves – they have neglected their own lives and personal potential as a result of their single-minded focus on business. What is needed both for the leaders of today and tomorrow is a focus not only on business, but also on life and leadership potential. When leaders focus on these three areas with a high-impact mentor to keep them accountable they can experience the outstanding outcome from leveraging their life, leadership, business and community.

THE 100X MODEL

This model focuses on four journeys: Life Journey, Leadership Journey, Business Journey and Community Journey. It has at its centre clarity of purpose. The key to the success of the model is the 100x leverage that comes from high-impact mentoring, teaching and advising to help you to get clarity and keep you accountable for implementing the processes that will help you to meet your purpose.

The compound effect of focusing on four areas simultaneously is phenomenal, as small changes in each area will produce great changes in all three cumulatively. The most important contribution is to help individuals challenge their paradigm and make a significant shift in taking specific actions to realise their purpose.

So, to leverage our lives, leadership, business and community 100x we need to begin with a purpose, a burning desire, a passionate dream, and the belief and faith to make it a reality. You need to begin working from the inside out and ensure that your life is given first priority.

LEVERAGING YOUR LIFE

Determine your life's purpose

- Commit to a burning desire and definite purpose for your life. Make it specific and set a date for achieving it. Recite this as a statement of commitment three to five times each day and believe that it will come to pass.

Become aware of what your strengths are

- Undertake specific tests to obtain feedback on your strengths, such as a personality profile, team role profile or Myers-Briggs profile.
- Seek feedback on your strengths from those who know you well.
- Investigate your past successes and study the patterns of your life by undertaking a two-day Life Planning exercise to identify and confirm your life direction and strengths.

Focus on your strengths

- Take your natural talents and become the best in the world.
- Don't do anything that is not in alignment with your strengths.
- Discover what you don't like doing and stop doing it.
- Delegate or ditch things that you cannot do well.
- Focus on the 80:20 rule – your top three most important priorities.

Leverage your time

- Practice self-management techniques by planning your ideal week, ideal month and ideal year based on your valued priorities.
- Plan daily, weekly, monthly and yearly – and review regularly.
- Allow time for spontaneous activities and new adventures.
- Always allow and book time each day for spiritual practices, personal exercise (weights, cardiovascular and stretching), good nutrition, important relationships, personal development, as well as time to relax and do something that you enjoy. Planning will help to prevent scheduling problems and ensure that you meet other high priority items.

Obtain a high-impact mentor

- A mentor will provide input and accountability to ensure that you take the priority actions that you are committed to.

There are many other aspects of leveraging your life, including: wealth creation; asset protection; tax planning; estate planning; spiritual development; family development; life transitions; personal interests; personal development; stress management; and nutritional management, all of which are part of an ongoing process of leveraging your life through a well planned and implemented Life Journey.

LEVERAGING YOUR LEADERSHIP

As you reflect on your life and articulate your purpose, your dreams and your reason for being, it will manifest itself in a passion, a calling, a direction and a grand design. As you gather momentum you will need to leverage your leadership so that you can multiply the potential 100x.

Clear vision

- In its simplest form, leadership is about the ability to get people to turn a vision into reality. It is critical that a leader focuses on having a clear vision, and taking massive action with great spirit.

Better future

- The one thing that great leaders focus on is rallying people toward a better future by discovering what is universal and capitalising on it. Universals of human nature include the fear of death, fear of people, fear of the future, fear of chaos and the fear of insignificance.

Meet the needs of people

- A leader needs to be able to meet the needs of people through focusing on their needs for security, community, clarity, authority and respect. When these needs are met they facilitate confidence, persistence, resilience and creativity.

Clarity

- Above all, leaders need to have clarity in and around whom they serve, what is their core strength and what is their core metric.

Taking massive action

- The major issue facing leaders today is the 'knowing-doing' gap. This is why mentoring is so important for leaders to ensure that the actions they plan are carried out.

Strategic thinking and judgment

- Leaders need to focus on strategic thinking and sound judgment. Related to this is the need to communicate their vision in an inspirational way so that people will follow and be committed to implementing it.

Ten disciplines of leadership

- As part of the Leadership Journey, leaders need to implement the ten disciplines of leadership:
- Take time to reflect.
- Be impeccable with your words toward your subconscious mind and others.
- Be aware of your assumptions.
- Do the best you can.
- Don't take things personally.
- Forgive yourself and others.
- Ask primary questions.
- Always act from thoughts and plans, rather than habit, to utilise your time wisely.
- Understand your impact on others.
- Be committed to developing as the art of leadership is the mastery of self.

Ultimately, leadership is the art of performance when the artist's instrument is 'self'. Mastery of 'self' is the secret of the art of leadership. So leveraging your development as a leader is related to implementing the ten disciplines of leadership in conjunction with a challenging mentor, teacher and adviser.

LEVERAGING YOUR BUSINESS

There are many aspects of business that could be considered, these are just a few:

Industry conditions

- It is important to evaluate the industry segments in which a company operates. Industry prospects and risks have a fundamental impact on a company's strategy and performance. Critical things to evaluate include industry life-cycle stage, competitive conditions, competitive advantage, opportunities and threats.

Strategic direction

- Use a process-oriented approach to articulate shareholders' purpose and direction, to identify where the company is, and to determine clear strategy for the future. Develop one-year business plans, budgeting and 90-day plans in conjunction with a Balanced Score Card and Key Performance Indicators (KPIs). The critical focus is for all managers, supervisors and staff to implement five key objectives every 90 days together with well-developed KPIs.

Internal capability

- Undertake a comprehensive evaluation of internal capability and implement actions in line with a financial plan, marketing plan, operational plan, human resource plan and technology plan.

Growth strategies

- If a company focuses on growing at 15 per cent per year, it will double every five years. To leverage a company, it will be necessary to explore other ways to grow, including differentiation, diversification, export, acquisitions, mergers and franchising, with appropriate risk assessment. Sources of equity funding will be important to enable this to occur.

Leadership and management capability

- One of the most critical factors for leveraging any company is the quality of management and staff. Extensive research has shown that many companies outgrow their senior management capability and falter. Equally important today is to be an employer of choice and be able to attract, engage and retain quality specialist staff. Related to that are the employment of Generation X and Y, the ageing Baby Boomer staff and the specific focus and needs of each group.

> Ultimately, leadership is the art of performance when the artist's instrument is 'self'.

When a person is impacted to change their life, leadership and business it can have a tremendous indirect impact on the community of their family, neighbourhood, local clubs, churches and community groups.

IMAGINE!

Imagine that you have undertaken a three to five-year process for the Life Journey, Leadership Journey, Business Journey and Community Journey. Can you imagine where you would be and what you would be doing? Imagine that you have become the excellent leader of other excellent leaders who have also leveraged their lives, and that you are running a very profitable, growing and leveraged business with satisfied staff, happy families and productive lives. And imagine what a great contribution that would be to the world.

"Nothing is more powerful than a person who knows their heart, and nothing is more unstoppable than a person who acts on that knowledge."

Life is a journey to abundance. No more and no less. And abundance is the contentment and joy that we experience when we do what we love. No more and no less. What I have discovered throughout my lifetime is that we either choose to create by picking up our paddle in the river of life, or we float aimlessly or destructively in its current. Either way, we will always hit rapids and tumble over falls, we may even get caught up in the endless circles of an eddy at the edge of life's river, but our experience will be totally different if we courageously pick up the oar. Our results are determined by our action and our inaction.

living abundantly
MAURICE GOLDBERG

THE ABUNDANCE MODEL

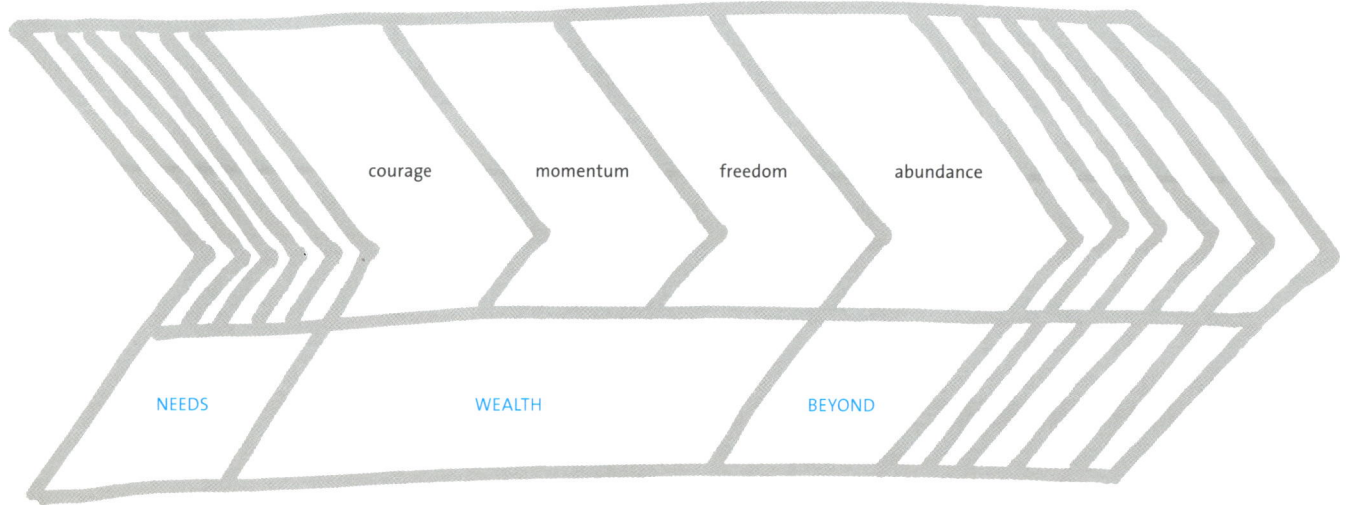

courage momentum freedom abundance

NEEDS WEALTH BEYOND

Do you ever ask yourself, "What's this life thing really all about?" Are we here to create extraordinary achievements or just to give birth to future generations? Do we all have the capacity to be a Mahatma Gandhi, Mother Teresa, Bill Gates or Anita Roddick? Is making a difference in the world, or being powerful or wealthy important? Or is the game really just about being happy? I've wondered about this for much of my life and I've regularly asked myself what really matters and what gives life meaning and purpose. What follows is a brief summary of what I've discovered about the journey to abundance.

There are four stages in the creation of a life of joy and contentment: courage, momentum, freedom and abundance. They are linear, that is they are achieved in that order and you cannot bypass any one of them. You'll no doubt recognise that you have lived these steps repeatedly throughout your life.

COURAGE

Let me begin by describing how I see most people living their lives: Adam lived in a town called Predictable on a lake called Known. He was very comfortable with his life, well, at least most of the time. He had a good job, nice friends, a comfortable house and got along fine with his family. Each day he would go out onto the lake in his canoe and do a few circuits. On occasions – and it seemed to be happening more and more often – a storm would come along and flood the lake. In fear of being swept out of the lake and into the River Unknown beyond, Adam would paddle ferociously against the current until he was exhausted. One afternoon, when just such a storm came along, something inside Adam

snapped. He stopped fighting the current. He stopped fighting his 'knowing' that there was more to life than the town called Predictable, and he courageously picked up his paddle and went with the flow of the storm toward the River Unknown.

Do you ever ask yourself, "What's this life thing really all about?"

The first step toward abundance is courage. We all ask ourselves, "Should I stay safe and unfulfilled in my life, reacting or responding to what others expect of me, or should I notice that there are other options and make a courageous stand for what I want, for what I would love to do?" It makes no difference whether you are a Mr or Ms Average, or a Super Achiever, you will probably still ask yourself these exact same questions, and feel the same pent up frustration that goes with them. When we feel the storms of discontent in our lives, we either bury them for fear of an unknown future or we accept the fear and courageously use our will to move toward something that we sense could be better.

The size of the storms over the lake called Known could have been significantly reduced if Adam had noticed the 'niggle'. His storms probably began as small irritants at first, such as boredom or loneliness. Then they may have developed into dissatisfaction and frustration. For some people the storm can get so bad that it develops into a near breakdown where there seems to be only two possible choices: to give in to the normality and numbness of life in the town called Predictable, or to do something radical in the realms of the unknown. When the first signs are niggles of possibility, it's so important to notice and not pretend they don't exist. Uncomfortable niggles, like grains of sand in an oyster, are the seeds of the pearls of our future happiness.

MOMENTUM

So, Adam left the town called Predictable and went into the River Unknown by taking courageous action. He believed he'd have a more abundant life, a life that felt free, and the gift of momentum propelled him forward.

When John F Kennedy decided in the early 1960s to send a man to the moon he took extraordinarily courageous action. This was a time in history when computers that filled entire rooms had less power than your iPod. There were no mobiles, no CDs, DVDs or even colour televisions. His was an outrageous promise that caused a radical shift in the pace of technological growth in the world and caused seemingly impossible consequences to become possible. It's the ease and speed with which these 'impossible consequences' unfold that encapsulates the character of the momentum stage. Kennedy's passionate declaration transformed our world socially, in terms of people's belief in what they could achieve; politically, in terms of increasing the vision of our leaders; and technologically, by achieving so much that had seemed impossible. Momentum is the gift we receive for taking courageous action.

Momentum makes change easy, it creates impossibly extraordinary outcomes, and its only real enemy is us! In the late 1990s, in my capacity as an investment adviser, I became particularly excited about a property investment adjacent to the Sydney Harbour Bridge. A week before its launch I only had one prospective client, but over the next ten days people literally came out of nowhere to buy. I even met one person in the lift of my apartment block who three hours later bought a $3 million penthouse. I ended up with 14 sales worth almost $25 million in less than two weeks.

My own courageous step was to believe that I could afford to buy one of these properties myself because I truly loved the location and believed it to be an amazing investment opportunity for anyone. The momentum that followed was 'impossible' to comprehend, and in the end it was my fear of what was happening – almost out of control success – that caused me to put on the breaks. I stopped the momentum, just as I'm sure you can think of times when you have squashed your own success or happiness without a logical reason.

FREEDOM

Whenever we focus on what we want there is an invisible force that pulls us forward and the momentum that follows our courageous action pushes us on toward what we want, toward what most people call 'freedom'. Freedom is what most people are reaching for.

In the world of wealth creation I see people set goals such as, "When I have the red Alfa sports I'll feel I've made it". "When I own an investment property I think I'll be nearly there." "When I pay off my home I know I'll be free!" But in fact, what happens after we have achieved our goal is that we eventually feel freedom dissipate and once more we search for what feels missing. We then go straight back to the beginning. We start at the first stage of courage again and this time create something bigger, a bit more dramatic, a bit more daring, a bit more creative. And whether it was your career or the next promotion, a nicer car, bigger home, new boat, giving the kids a better education, or maybe even an overseas education…the cycle of courage, momentum and freedom just repeats itself over and over again, like 'Groundhog Day', as we strive to create more and more in the search for sustained freedom.

But freedom never comes and we begin to realise that what we believed we would create through achieving our desires was an illusion. This is when people start to ask the bigger questions about their lives. It's like moving from the town called Predictable to the City called Why?! People get to the point where they think, I'm wealthy and have a nice home and all these nice 'things', and they give up, or give in, or escape to the countryside or to a simpler life. Others leave the workforce or give up on a marriage that had 'real potential'. In fact what people do is give up because it's too hard to endlessly keep creating more and more in search of happiness. They are addicted to the need to keep searching for freedom. Freedom is a drug, an opiate, and it's never going to give us what we want because the truth is that we are never really looking for freedom. We are on the wrong river, going in the wrong direction! What we are really looking for is contentment. Peace and joy. Happiness. Abundance.

There is a simple secret to getting what we really want, to finding abundance. But until we have dared to create courageously, and experienced the frustration of 'Groundhog Day' – of creating over and over again in the quest for freedom – we won't be ready to explore the path to abundance.

ABUNDANCE

So what is the secret? What is the way to abundance? It is simply to get clear that what we so courageously want to create is something that we love! It's that simple! But most people get confused and create what they *think* they love, or what they *think* they need, or what they *think* they want – but it's not what they would really love in their lives.

There are three options for all people when we create our lives. The first is that we create because we fear something. We respond to that fear and keep on repeating the same paths to supposed happiness: when I escape my fears I will be happy. The second is that we create because we desire. We are attracted like a moth to a flame: when I get what I desire I will be happy.

It's interesting how these powerful forces of fear and desire have been recognised for so long. When looking at the biblical story of the Garden of Eden, the garden was the place of abundance and the only thing keeping mankind out of this paradise were two angels (or cherubs) that guarded its gates. One of these was the angel of fear and the other was the angel of desire; it is only possible to pass through the gates of abundance when man is not motivated by fear or desire. It is the third option for creating our lives that lets us pass into Eden, and that is by asking ourselves what do we really love? What do we really stand for? What do we really want? And, what are we truly passionate about?

When I think of great people who have lived abundantly, I think of Gandhi and Mother Teresa; I think of Anita Roddick and Richard Branson; I think of Moses and Jesus, Mohammed and Buddha; I think of many extraordinary loving mothers and fathers; and I think of people who courageously follow their truth, not those focused on being famous or powerful. To choose 'power' is to fear feeling powerless. The leaders of war in our world choose control and power. They follow their desires and run from their fears. They believe they are heading toward 'freedom', but they are really reliving their own private *'Groundhog Day'* and becoming the victim of their own fears and desires.

CREATING YOUR OWN ABUNDANT LIFE

So, you may be wondering, where do I start? Or how does this work for a business, a government, a religion – or in your own life? It all starts at the same place. Ask yourself what you really love doing. What is it that lights you up? It has nothing to do with forces outside of yourself and nothing to do with other people or their ideas, for they just tie into the insecurities that prevent you from going forward and creating what you love.

In 1989 I came across a life-changing exercise. It was at the end of a very frustrating period of my life. I had just responded to a big storm over the town of Predictable – I had quit my job in architecture and was lost on a new river between careers. I travelled to New York and decided that if I walked the streets, read all the 'right' books and made space to ponder, I would return home two months later with all the answers. I had very little money, a mortgage, no relationship and no idea what I really wanted in my life. Well, most of the books still sit on my bookshelf, unread, but two hours with a pen in my hand doing this exercise changed the way I saw the world.

The instructions read: Take a few hours and sit in a place where there will be no interruptions. Pick up a pen and a few clean sheets of paper and start writing. Write about the moment – the exact second – before you die. Write about the temperature, the smells, the sounds, what you see in the few metres around you. Where are you? What are you doing? What age are you? What colour is the sky? Is there anyone there?

Ask yourself what you really love doing – what is it that lights you up?

I spent the next 40 minutes writing about the last few moments of my life. I was in my early nineties, in my garden, on the terrace of a wharf penthouse adjacent to the Sydney Harbour Bridge. It was a beautiful day. Then I wrote about the previous few hours, and then the previous few days, and finally the whole week. I had so many people I loved and who loved me in my life, both at home and in business. I still worked mentoring creative professionals. I was confident, at ease, joyous, totally content – I guess you could say I had an abundant life! I then spent the next hour going backward in time joining the future to the present. And somehow my subconscious mind got the message – the message of who I really am and what is important to me. I guess I started to understand the difference between choosing a life of 'supposed' freedom and one where I could truly create what I love.

In my role as someone who helps people build wealth and prosperity I have come to realise that in this world where there is so much discrepancy between rich and poor, happy and sad, the rich can be sad and the poor can be happy. Abundance can live as much in the gutter as it can in a mansion. Abundance is a state of mind that does not discriminate based on race, religion or financial means.

As I work with my clients I'm aware of their 'needs' – a house, a car, a good education for their children and a comfortable retirement. You could say that they want 'everything covered'. As we move forward with their goals 'wealth' is usually their next objective, that is, to be able to afford what you want when you want it. The outcome of this stage is that 'anything is possible'. But without the third stage, as human beings journeying on the river of life, our life's possibilities seem underutilised, our brief journey here becomes wasted – a life half lived. So 'needs' are the base level and 'wealth' may follow, but the third stage, 'beyond wealth' is what interests me most.

'Beyond wealth' is where you find joy, probably happiness and possibly even abundance – and it is certainly a time when life is remarkable! To go 'beyond wealth' you must keep creating the life of your dreams, by creating the things that light you up, that give you goose bumps, that make your heart sing and that bring you and those around you abundance.

Life is too short to be a victim, to courageously yet habitually create without real meaning and to ignore the intensity of our spirit that gives us so much purpose. So, courageously create with meaning and purpose and live the life that each of us has hidden inside. For nothing is more powerful than a person who knows their heart, and nothing is more unstoppable than a person who acts on that knowledge.

SO, HOW DO I BEGIN TO LIVE AN ABUNDANT LIFE?

Below are some simple actions that you can take right now, that will immediately cause transformation in your life. Choose any one of the statements each day and make it your mantra for 24 hours. Notice how easy or difficult it is to stick with your decision to change your behaviour and thoughts. Don't give up! Persist! You will notice significant change even after only a few days.

STATEMENT	HINTS
Courage	
"I feel the fear and do it anyway."	Fear will always exist.
"I listen to my niggles."	These irritants are the pearls of your future.
"I use my will."	It only takes a decision to switch you into action.
Momentum	
"I let momentum flow."	You are the only one who can stop it.
"Momentum is a gift."	Enjoy it, don't reject it.
Freedom	
"I love what I'm doing."	Are you responding to fear and/or a desire?
"Why am I doing this?"	If it's not something you love, it's probably a habit. Stop doing it now!
"I'm becoming aware of my addictions."	What am I addicted to? Is it driven by fear and/or desire?
"I am completely at choice."	You have free will no matter what anyone says.
Abundance	
"I do what I love."	When you do what you love everyone is always a winner (even if it doesn't seem so at first).
"I love what I do."	Life is not always easy but joy and contentment will come from doing what you love.

"One of the greatest myths about creating wealth is that you have to earn a high income – the truth is it's not how much you earn but what you do with it that matters."

The great Australian dream is to own your own home and be debt-free, which many people do achieve after 20 years of diligence and hard work. But paying off your mortgage is not necessarily the fastest way to become debt-free. In fact, if you want to pay off your home faster, it's actually better to borrow more money, not less.

making more from less
CHRIS GRAY

LEVERAGE YOUR WAY TO WEALTH

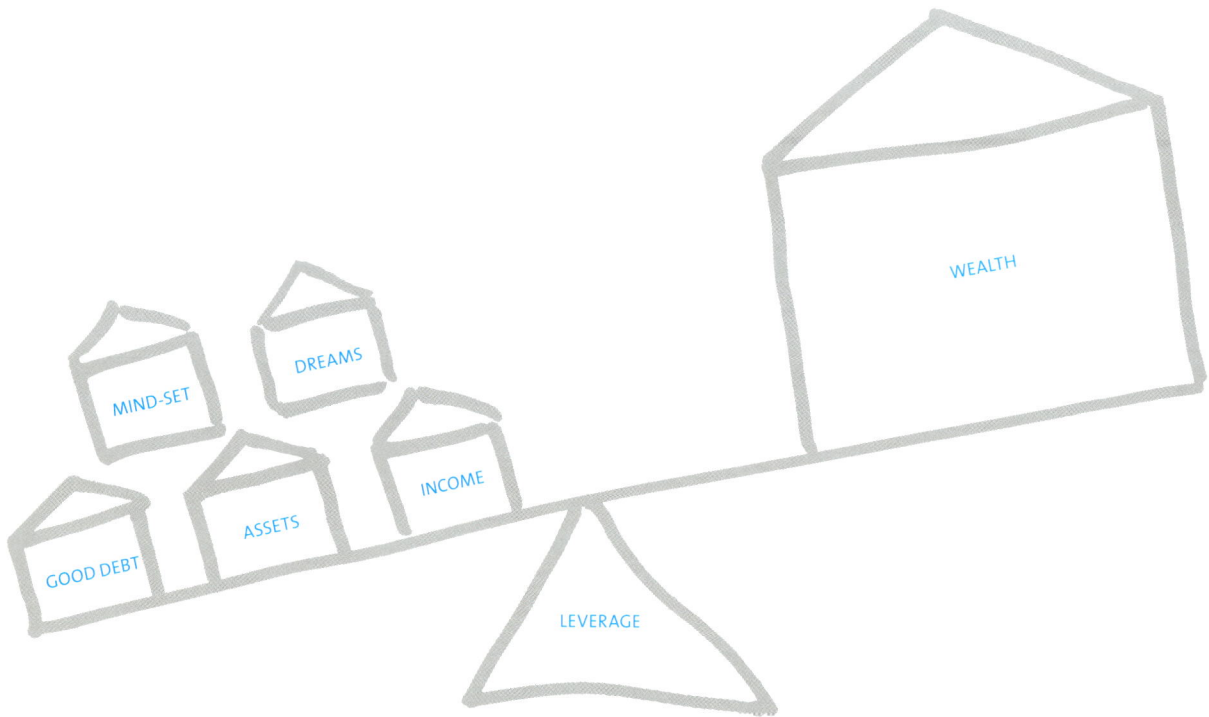

MIND-SET

DREAMS

GOOD DEBT

ASSETS

INCOME

LEVERAGE

WEALTH

The government and lending institutions are so conservative that they would never recommend it, and in principle it does all seem to make sense: take a 25 or 30 year mortgage, pay it off and reduce your outgoings. It's what conventional wisdom says, and it's what everyone does. But I don't believe they have thought it through mathematically.

RESIDENTIAL PROPERTY DOUBLES IN VALUE EVERY SEVEN YEARS

Somehow, most people forget to weigh in the fact that according to long-term average statistics, residential property tends to double in value every seven years. The average Sydney property, which is worth $520,000 today, was worth $16,000 in 1969. A good property in a high-growth area will probably increase in value even faster. Take a look around at your parents' home, and even among your circle of friends, and note how much their properties have gone up. Compare that figure with how much you can potentially save from working – there is no contest.

If you bought a property right now for $300,000, according to the 'Seven-Year Rule' it should appreciate at the following rate:

YEARS	PROPERTY
0	$300k
7	$600k
14	$1.2m
21	$2.4m
28	$4.8m

$4.8 million may sound like an unrealistic figure but if you apply the numbers to your parents' or grandparents' first property, you will see that history confirms this trend. Many people over-analyse the market, especially the little ups and downs that the newspapers tend to highlight. The key is to concentrate on the five to 10-year picture and make sure you have enough of a cash flow buffer to see you through any short-term tremors.

ASSETS INCREASE FASTER THAN YOU CAN SAVE

It's shocking but true – earning a high income may not make you rich! Have you noticed how as your salary has gone up over the years so too has the amount that you spend? Rather than creating more wealth over time, most people actually create more debt. And rather than creating good debt (to buy investment property) it is usually bad debt (flash cars and holidays).

> Have you noticed how as your salary has gone up over the years so too has the amount that you spend? Rather than creating more wealth over time, most people actually create more debt.

A lot of people think one way to get ahead is by getting a pay rise or a bonus, but the figures don't stack up. Let's consider a big pay rise, for example $20,000 per year. You can immediately cut it in half because tax eats up the first $10,000, and the rest will level out at slightly less than $1,000 per month in your pocket. And an extra $1,000 per month certainly isn't going to make you rich. All it will do is allow you to eat at slightly better restaurants, wear slightly better clothes and drive a slightly better car. And how often can you hope for a whopping $20,000 pay rise?

It's not how much you earn, it's what you do with it that counts. How can you use your limited income to make more money? The simple principle is if you buy something that is increasing in value by 10 per cent per annum with a 10 per cent deposit, you will double your money in the first 12 months. For example, if $10,000 buys a $100,000 asset, and that asset is worth $110,000 12 months later, your $10,000 investment will increase in value to $20,000. Whether you pay off the remaining $90,000 is irrelevant as it is the increase in the asset value that makes the money, not repaying the debt. Making money by borrowing other people's money is called *leveraging*.

Consider this example. If you bought a property for $400,000 which appreciated by a conservative 25 per cent over four years, its new value of $500,000 would be the equivalent of saving $25,000 per year. How many people can save $25,000 a year from their wages? Very few.

Property is great for leveraging time and money. Most of us understand residential investments because we all live in one, and the rent and capital growth returns are usually more stable than the alternatives such as a share portfolio, for example. Having bought a property it pretty much looks after itself, and it will never fall to zero value, as the land is always worth something. The same cannot be said about shares, collectible art, commodity futures, or other investment alternatives.

ADVANTAGES OF PAYING OFF LESS

Our parents' generation has made a lot of money from property over the past 30 years, but it's obvious now that they would be in an even better financial position if they had concentrated on buying even just one additional property, rather than trying to pay off their mortgage.

Consider this: if rather than paying off your mortgage you used the capital element of your repayments to purchase another property, it should also double in value every seven years.

Let's assume that you borrow 100 per cent of the purchase costs and buy two $300,000 properties with a total mortgage of $600,000. The following figures represent the equation at the time of purchase:

	HOME	HOME + INVESTMENT
Property	$300k	$600k
Mortgage	($300k)	($600k)
Equity	0	0

However, in 14 years' time, the equation will look like this:

	HOME	HOME + INVESTMENT
Property	$1.2m	$2.4m
Mortgage	($200k)	($600k)
Equity	$1m	$1.6m

These numbers suggest that you can make more money by buying a second property than you can by saving the interest on what you pay off.

Realise that the amount you are paying in mortgage repayments is minute in comparison with the appreciation of your property. So while it would take seven years for your initial property to double in value, having a second property means you are making twice the profit.

Buying two properties rather than one may appear to be a bit more risky on day one, but as soon as you get some growth you create equity much faster. In the first situation you will have probably paid $100,000 off your loan and made $900,000 in capital gain, yielding a total profit of $1 million. Whereas in the second scenario you've paid nothing off your loan but have made $1.6 million in capital gain so you're $600,000 better off. You do need to take rent and other costs into account but these items are relatively insignificant when you consider the big picture. The better you buy in the first place, the more instant equity you create. This equity can be used as a buffer zone to help you cash flow any difference between the rent and your expenses.

I believe that it is better to concentrate on making another million than it is to worry about being tax efficient on $300,000. I would rather have $3.5 million in property and $3.5 million in debt (no equity) than have a fully paid off $1 million home, because at some point in time my $3.5 million will double to $7 million; whereas double $1 million is only $2 million.

LEVERAGING YOUR WAGES

I bought my first property at the age of 22 and the numbers that I saw did not add up. Conventional thinking of buying a one-bedroom unit, which was just about affordable, would have enslaved me for the rest of my life paying off that mortgage. Whereas by thinking differently and buying a three-bedroom house, which was not affordable according to my wages, I could be almost mortgage free if I rented the two spare rooms to friends.

PROPERTY TYPE	ONE-BED UNIT	THREE-BED HOUSE
Cost in 1992	125,000	200,000
Rent	0	750
Mortgage	(521)	(911)
Cost to me / mth	(521)	(161)
Capital gain/yr @ 10%	12,500	20,000

By getting a mortgage seven times my income, rather than the usual three, not only was a three-bedroom house cheaper to run than a one-bedroom unit, but it also gave me an extra 60 per cent in capital gain. At 22, I had to turn up to work 40-plus hours a week to earn $25,000 (less tax and super) whereas by doing virtually nothing I could earn $20,000 from a property.

Even if you're earning a $100,000-$150,000 per year salary, you've generally got to work hard, usually from 7.00am-7.00pm, five – possibly even seven – days per week. Compare this effort with having a $1-$1.5 million property asset that is increasing by $100,000-$150,000 in a single year, where you don't really have to do anything except buy well, and meet a dozen repayments.

NEVER SELL

Of all of the things I have learnt over the years, the one that surprised me most is the realisation that you don't actually ever have to sell your current property in order to buy more. If you bought well in the first place, why sell it? In fact, buying and selling – or selling and buying – will cost you possibly between 10 and 35 per cent of the property value, which could be most of the money you stand to make. I have never sold and I never intend to. But I've seen many people regret selling properties when they realise that they could have made so much more profit by hanging on to them, because you can always borrow against existing property. In fact, you can borrow and buy more property by using the existing property as collateral. And remember, the collateral value of every property you buy increases every year that passes.

CHALLENGING WHAT YOU'VE DONE IN THE PAST

Often, what has happened in the past is a good indicator of what will happen in the future. If you evaluate what you have done in the last ten years and then visualise, based on that, where you will be in the next ten years, will you be happy? Often we think that by working hard all of our financial dreams will come true, but do they really? I don't think so. If you want your future to be different from your past, something has to *change*.

Higher incomes don't always guarantee greater wealth and they generally bring more stress and time away from home. Learning how to leverage your limited income will give you a better monetary result with not a lot of extra effort.

"Strong leadership is the number one motivator for Generations X and Y – yet many organisations have not invested in developing their leadership capabilities for decades."

Peter Drucker, in a book titled *The Leader of the Future*, observed that '…there may be born leaders, but there surely are too few to depend on them. Leadership must be learned and can be learned'. My personal belief, after working in human resources for 12 years, is that leadership is a set of learnable behaviours, which can be adopted and modelled by observing leaders who exhibit ethical behaviours and strong values – qualities that 'followers' admire and respect.

leadership across the generations
AVRIL HENRY

LEADERSHIP EXPECTATIONS ACROSS GENERATIONS

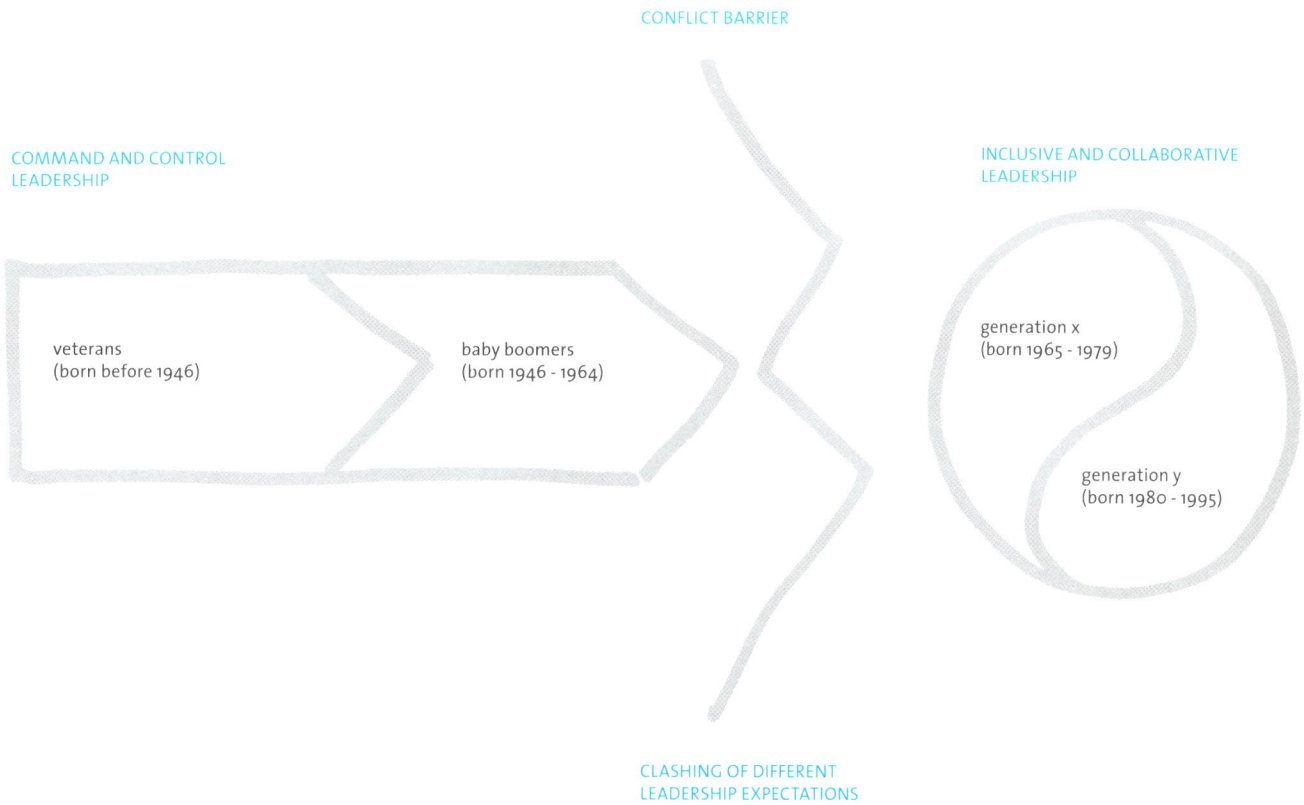

CONFLICT BARRIER

COMMAND AND CONTROL
LEADERSHIP

INCLUSIVE AND COLLABORATIVE
LEADERSHIP

veterans
(born before 1946)

baby boomers
(born 1946 - 1964)

generation x
(born 1965 - 1979)

generation y
(born 1980 - 1995)

CLASHING OF DIFFERENT
LEADERSHIP EXPECTATIONS

Unfortunately, many Australian organisations have not invested in developing management and leadership capability for decades. It is widely believed that these are 'soft skills' and therefore not as important as technical skills and work experience. Soft skills have long been seen as an unnecessary overhead and are considered to be readily expendable during the annual budgeting cycle when cost reductions are needed. But ironically, strong leadership is the number one motivator for the two youngest generations in our workforce – Generation X (born 1965-1979) and Generation Y (born 1980-1995) – who comprise approximately 59 per cent of Australian workplaces. Their principal loyalty is not to the organisation, but to their own careers and to a good manager. The absence of strong leadership and a good manager is the number one reason why many Generation X and Y employees leave organisations.

When asked what 'good leadership' means, Generation X say it is 'leaders who do what they say they will do'; Generation Y, who are impatient by nature, extend this to include '…when they say they will do it!'

In a research report on Generation Y titled, *The Who, What, When and Y of Generation whY?*, over 75 per cent of participants identified the most important characteristics of effective leadership, in order of importance, as:
• an ability to inspire and motivate people
• being a good listener
• creating a positive work environment
• leading by example.

Other leadership characteristics they rated highly include:
• valuing teamwork
• an ability to manage change
• having good values
• demonstrating self-leadership
• an appetite for learning and developing others
• coaching and mentoring.

Based on the fact that many Generation Y employees have not been in the workplace that long, and that they have different expectations of the workplace and their managers, the participants were asked to think about the best team leader or manager they had worked for, and what it was that made them such a good manager. Overwhelmingly, the majority of participants said it was that person's ability to listen to staff. This was closely followed by managers who treat all people with respect and as equals, and who do not regard themselves as 'superior' to the people they are responsible for managing. Included in the top characteristics of a good manager, were also:
• giving regular and constructive feedback
• explaining things
• answering questions and coaching staff
• being encouraging and supportive.

These young Australian workers identified a total of 14 characteristics of a good manager from their perspective. Ironically, many of these are not considered to be as important as technical expertise, experience and tertiary qualifications by the two older generations who make up the majority of senior management positions in both the public and private sectors.

This strong desire of Australian employees for good leadership is further supported by the Hewitt Best Employers in Australia studies conducted by Hewitt Associates over the last five years. These have identified the number one factors that set organisations apart as being strong leadership and a commitment to the people inside the organisation.

Currently, approximately 80 per cent of board and senior management positions in Australia are occupied by Veterans (born prior to 1946) and Baby Boomers (born 1946-1964), who have a different understanding of the key motivators for the two younger generations.

In broad terms, Australian leaders fail in the following key areas:
• managing poor performance in the workplace
• giving regular and constructive feedback
• listening skills
• exhibiting command and control leadership styles.

Australian managers and leaders do not like giving feedback, and are even more uncomfortable receiving feedback on their own performance from their subordinates. They do not like giving feedback on poor performance because it upsets people. Studies by Human Synergistics International have found that Australian leaders have the highest level of 'avoidance leadership' in the world. This is characterised by fear of engagement, withdrawal from taking responsibility and a preference to defer decision making. At the other end of the feedback scale, we find Australian leaders promoting the tall poppy syndrome; that is, 'we can't tell people when they are doing a good job in case they 'get up themselves". So Australian employees are left with no feedback at all! This is unacceptable to Generations X and Y, who not only expect feedback, but will demand it. They want to know when they are doing well so they can continue to do it. But they also want to know when they are not doing well, what they need to do to improve and what their leader or manager is willing to do to help them.

The Hewitt Best Employers in Australia studies have found that leaders in those organisations are strong communicators, good listeners, and open and honest in their communication style. One of the most valuable leadership lessons I've learnt was from my maternal grandmother who told me when I became school captain that it was important to listen in order to be effective in my first leadership role. She said, "God gave us two ears and one mouth because He expected us to listen more than He expected us to speak!" A simple but powerful lesson.

One can learn a lot more about our people and our workplaces by listening more and talking less, by observing in silence and listening with our ears, eyes and hearts. One of the qualities of highly effective leaders is that they don't believe that they have all the answers themselves. They recognise that the answers to many workplace issues may be found within the organisation and often at levels below management. They ask questions of employees at all levels, and willingly listen to their contributions. This earns respect for the leader, but also demonstrates respect by the leader for the employees. In order to engage the employees, the leader must help them understand why they must follow, rather than just assume that they will follow.

In order to move toward a more collaborative and inclusive leadership style, leaders need to focus on:

- Learning how to give and receive constructive feedback about both good and poor performance.
- Building learning cultures within organisations and enabling the development of management and leadership skills in all employees responsible for leading and managing others.
- Creating positive work environments, where employees are encouraged to be the best they can be.
- Adopting more inclusive approaches to problem solving by seeking input from employees, where possible.
- Moving from command and control leadership to more collaborative, inclusive leadership.

In the late 1990s two forward-thinking men, David Clancy and Robert Webber, wrote a book titled *Roses and Rust* which was about redefining the essence of leadership in a new age. It challenged traditional assumptions about organisations, management and our most valued resource in business, people. What resonated most with me was their description of people who would challenge the status quo in organisations, whom they referred to as 'Pioneers of Hope'. These people work tirelessly to re-establish hope and create positive work environments to ensure that work has meaning for people, and to create a bright working future for generations to come. They are determined to walk the path of the 'unsayables' and hold up mirrors within their organisations, or those of their clients, so that organisations can grow and move forward ethically. It is people such as these that truly inspire others to be the best they can be, and show others the way things could be in the future, rather than just how they are at present. This is what Generations X and Y are looking for in their leaders: people who are ethical, honest, trustworthy and courageous, who want to create a better work environment for the present and the future.

In order for a leader to be truly credible, he or she needs to lead by example, exhibiting appropriate behaviours in his or her own life. In the words of Father Chris Riley, CEO of Youth Off The Streets: "Leading by example is how leaders make vision and values tangible. It is how they provide evidence that they're personally committed. And that evidence is what people look for and admire in leaders – people whose direction they willingly follow".

"Growing up without a father, becoming a parent at 19 and declaring bankruptcy at 24 are just a few of the things I don't remember writing on my life's 'to do' list."

Every experience, every moment in life provides us with opportunities and choices. And how we respond determines our eventual level of success, prosperity and happiness. Although we may not be able to control all the events of our lives, we can control our actions. When life happens, we can choose to either become bitter or better, to hinder or help others. We can choose to hang onto the past or we can let go and look forward to a future of opportunities. In other words, we can choose to either be Worriers or Warriors.

from worrier to warrior
SHANE KEMPTON

WORRIER VS WARRIOR MODEL

A WORRIER'S LIFE-CYCLE

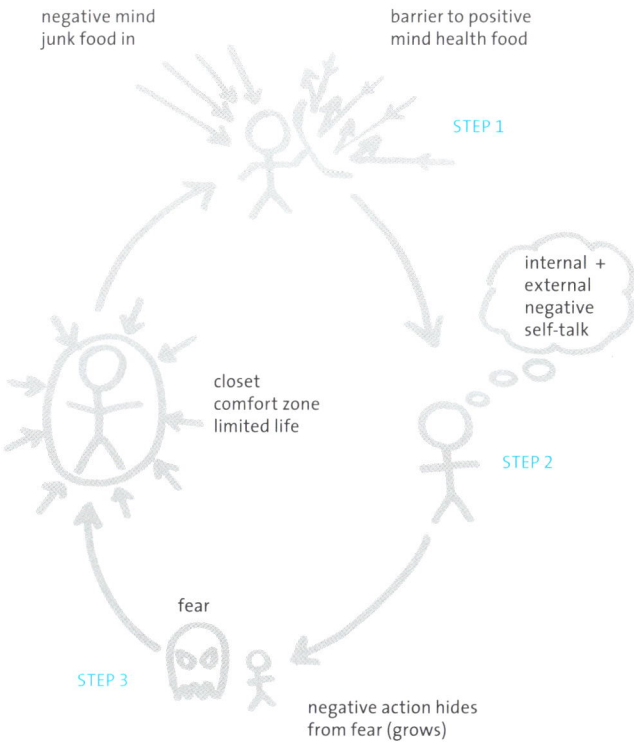

negative mind
junk food in

barrier to positive
mind health food

STEP 1

internal +
external
negative
self-talk

closet
comfort zone
limited life

STEP 2

fear

STEP 3

negative action hides
from fear (grows)

A WARRIOR'S LIFE-CYCLE

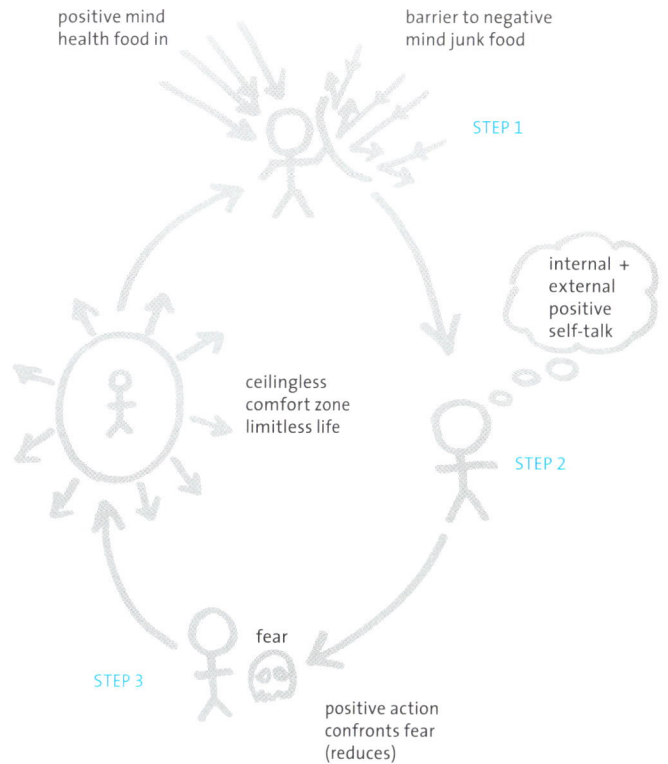

positive mind
health food in

barrier to negative
mind junk food

STEP 1

internal +
external
positive
self-talk

ceilingless
comfort zone
limitless life

STEP 2

fear

STEP 3

positive action
confronts fear
(reduces)

The Warrior metaphor immediately creates a mental image of a person who is confident and courageous, yet selfless. A person who is generous and whose moral character is built upon integrity and values; a person who is never rushed, and who always makes time for what is important, not necessarily what is urgent; a person with a purpose to help people and do the right thing. In fact, a person with the very same character traits found in all successful and prosperous people.

At the age of 30, I made a decision to stop thinking and reacting to life like a Worrier, and to start living a life of purpose, like a Warrior. It was a decision that had a profound effect on both my personal and business life. During the next six years, I went from being a soldier in the army to becoming a multi award-winning real estate sales consultant, the owner of Australia's number one real estate office, and the CEO of one of Australia's biggest real estate groups. Now don't get me wrong, just because I made the decision to become a Warrior did not automatically mean that success flowed freely to me. What it did do was trigger the beginning of a journey of continual improvement and a commitment to live a life of success, prosperity and happiness.

Although living the life of a Warrior is an ongoing process of learning and growth, there are three simple things that you can implement immediately that will have a positive and profound effect on your life as you start your journey down the path of becoming a Warrior.

• Feed your mind the right food
• Whatever you say goes
• Beware of comfort zones

FEED YOUR MIND THE RIGHT FOOD: A WARRIOR UNDERSTANDS THAT THEIR EXTERNAL WORLD IS A MIRROR OF THEIR INTERNAL WORLD.

All things in life are created twice: first as an idea or dream, and second, in reality. You see, all our inner thoughts, whether negative or positive, eventually manifest into reality. What you think about and focus your mind on determines your external behaviors and thus creates the environment that validates your internal thoughts. Knowing this Universal Law to be true, it makes sense to ensure that we feed our minds with the right foods. A poor mind-diet creates far bigger challenges than a poor food diet.

Every experience, every moment in life provides us with opportunities and choices. And how we respond to these opportunities determines our eventual level of success, prosperity and happiness.

There are some very real similarities between our stomachs and our minds. They both need food in order to function; plant and animal material being the food for our stomachs, and knowledge and positive energy being the food for our minds. Both will accept good and bad food, but both will perform better when filled with the right foods.

The biggest difference between our stomachs and our minds is that we can never overfill our minds with too much good food or energy. Our minds have a constant craving, but they're not fussy about what we feed them, whether positive or negative, so we must be responsible and ensure (like we do with our stomachs) that we only feed our minds with positive energy. If we become careless, we can go on a mental 'junk food' binge and absorb any and all of the negative energy that surrounds us every day in this fast and furious world.

The only way I know to limit the amount of 'stinking thinking' that I let into my life is by ensuring that my mind is constantly full of positive energy and knowledge, and that I associate with people who complement the positive lifestyle that I want to live.

WHAT YOU SAY GOES: A WARRIOR UNDERSTANDS THAT WHETHER YOU SAY YOU CAN, OR SAY YOU CANNOT, YOU'RE RIGHT!

There is an alarming amount of self-defeating language spoken, muttered and thought by Worriers every day. How often have you heard people say things like, "I can't lose weight," or "This job is giving me grey hair," or "I can't save money," or "I don't have enough time to exercise," or one of the worst ones, "This relationship is killing me". The list of negative programming statements goes on and on. And what's worst of all is that generally these statements come true for these people.

We have all seen the results that negative self-talk can bring, so start becoming aware of what you are saying and programming yourself with. Here is a simple example of the results that a subtle change in your self-talk can achieve. Want to rid your life of problems? Warriors do not have any problems; I'll show you why.

Every day, people say things like, "I have a PROBLEM with my kids," or "This guy at my work is a real PROBLEM," or "I have a PROBLEM with this project".

By simply swapping the word PROBLEM with CHALLENGE, you put a positive spin on a potentially negative situation. Warriors understand this and they carefully choose their words to ensure that their language complements their positive objectives.

Here is an example of what I have been saying to myself since I learnt the power of positive self-talk many years ago:

"I am a HAPPY, GIVING, FIT and HEALTHY, WEALTHY, SUCCESSFUL, YOUNG, LOYAL, PROUD, AUSTRALIAN, FAMILY MAN, with inspirational LEADERSHIP and MENTORING skills who generates a fantastic six-figure per year income for my family through my real estate business, books, CDs and workshops."

I say it when I feel down to pick myself up, I say it when I am driving in my car, and I say it before I go to bed at night.

BEWARE OF COMFORT ZONES: A WARRIOR UNDERSTANDS THAT GOOD CAN GET IN THE WAY OF GREAT.

Our comfort zone is the place where we are right now. It is the place and state of mind in which we exist. It may be in our job, our career, our company or in our relationships. No matter where they are, we are defined by our comfort zones.

We think that we're safe in our comfort zone. We do what we are comfortable with and if we don't challenge ourselves, so what? We are safe there, we are happy there. We're getting along nicely, so why change anything?

What happened to all those dreams and ambitions you once had? When was it that you decided to become a Worrier, to settle for average and to not reach for your true Warrior potential? I certainly don't remember ever saying, "I'll settle for less and be a Worrier".

Many of us foolishly let ourselves be dictated to by society and negative media; we begin to think like Worriers and to accept that our dreams, ambitions and potential will never be fully realised. We pretend that we are happy, but in fact we are lying to ourselves.

Stop and think about your comfort zone. You can't physically see the boundaries, but you can feel them. It's like an invisible line in the sand that stops us from moving. Yet beyond that line is the place where we will find our full potential. Worriers don't dare to go there, they tell themselves that they are not worthy or that they don't deserve it. The truth is that they are afraid and the only thing holding them back is their fear. Yet fear is not real. Fear is 'False Expectations Appearing Real'. It exists only in our imaginations.

The only way to break free from limiting comfort zones of fear is to confront them. As many wise scribes have written, the more you hide from your fears the worse and more daunting they become. Confront your fears and see what happens. They start to melt away, to retreat, to become smaller and more insignificant. Confront your fears and expand your comfort zone and you will find yourself in a new space where there are more opportunities.

Transforming yourself from being a Worrier to a Warrior involves the same process as achieving success, prosperity and happiness in life. It is not a singular event but a journey of continual growth and learning. Choose today to begin travelling the path of the Warrior and enjoy the gifts and opportunities in every moment that life gives you.

"Being a leader requires a total awareness of who you are inside and out, and the ability to take control of the perception you want people to have of you."

In today's world, leadership is all about perception. As a leader, are you in control of the impression you make on people? Do people 'get' what you are about and what you stand for? People are a puzzle, and as long as the pieces do not fit perfectly, the picture will always be incomplete. Consider the Mona Lisa without her smile, or Michelangelo's David with one; that simple, seemingly unimportant touch of difference would reduce the impact and worth of both works of art. So too, just one piece of the puzzle slightly out of place can diminish your leadership value.

identity management
OKSANA KORIAKOVA

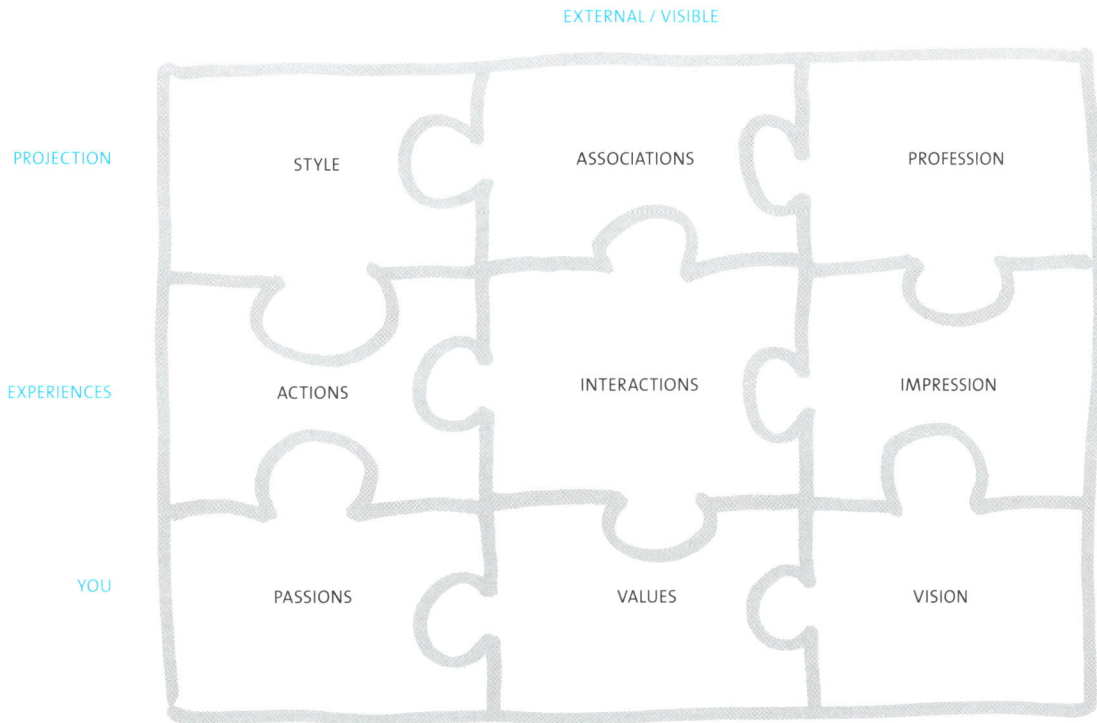

Today, the most persuasive leader is the one whose external perception is congruent with their inner identity. We are constantly making impressions and statements about who we are to others – often it happens before we even realise that we are doing so, and without careful management, it can result in the person we present ourselves to be, being incongruent with the value systems we really hold. There are three layers through which we are all assessed, both consciously and subconsciously, by the people around us: projection, experiences and you.

PROJECTION

This is the introductory level where you are 'judged' by your image, your profession and the associations you keep. If you find that people often have an incorrect first impression of you, this is most likely the area you will need to assess and fix. Fortunately, because it is only the external manifestation of you as a leader, rather than something more fundamental about who you are, it is quite easy to work with. Let's briefly look at each of the elements of projection.

Your style: This is about what you wear, how you wear it, what you own and how you present yourself physically. Every one of these 'things' is relevant to the impression people have of you. People will judge you before they have even said hello on the basis of how you are physically presented.

The old adage 'clothes maketh the man' is even more relevant in this day and age when snap judgements are being made constantly, especially of our leaders. Imagine if John Howard were to meet with another head of state wearing a tailored Italian suit, but with unpolished shoes and a Mickey Mouse tie. His first impression on that dignitary would immediately be devalued – and you can be sure that the press would have a field day discussing that image error!

Fortunately, style can be learnt and it can be created uniquely for you to ensure that the first impression you make is consistent with the person you believe yourself to be.

Your associations: This is a large category that includes such associations as where you are from, the clubs or networks you belong to, the sports you play and watch, the friends you keep company with, and who your family is. Some of these things are also among the first few questions asked in most introductory conversations.

While there may be some associations that cannot be changed, it is important that you understand the statement and image that each of your associations makes about you. There may be areas that can be modified, supplemented or enhanced to ensure that you are in control of the impression people will have of you.

Your profession: This is about what you do, and would have to be the most frequently asked question after your name. As human beings, our brains have the instinctive need to categorise people; to fit them into a little niche that we can create a set of expectations around. What is your immediate mental picture of the types of people you would expect to find in the following professions: lawyer, accountant, waitress, HR manager, real estate agent? It's important to understand that your profession is the external perception that people will have of you.

You can choose your profession; you can change your career. Where you are now is not your destiny but a role that you may have decided to get into when you were a teenager. Surely, that 18-year-old is not still making decisions for you?

EXPERIENCES

This area of perception comes from a greater level of interaction with you. As people get to 'experience' you, they get to know you better and their first impressions of you may change. Experiences include actions, interactions and impressions.

Your actions: This refers to people's indirect experience of you. It might be that they have heard of something you have done through someone else, or watched you do something that they themselves were not directly involved in. Either way, every move you make is watched, assessed and stored in their memories for evaluation, either immediately or at a later time.

Your interactions: These take place through your direct involvement with others. For example, you may be at a business dinner with someone, or at a party together, and how you behave after a few drinks, in a larger social group, or how you speak with each person there will have a direct impact on the impressions you are creating in people's minds.

Your impressions: These are ongoing impressions you can make without actually being involved face-to-face. For example, you might send a note of thanks to the host of a party, or an email to acknowledge the people you met at a networking function recalling individual personal details about them. The impression you create after your actions and interactions is just as important as the direct impact you have on the people you encounter.

YOU

Finally, there's you. That complex being with subtle nuances that even you are not aware of, made up of a myriad of genetic and environmental influences. We could really delve into the whole psychology of 'you', but for now the real understanding we need to have is who you are in terms of the values you hold (as a result of, or perhaps even in spite of your experiences), where you are right now in terms of your general attitude, the passions you have, where you see yourself in the future and the unique vision that you want to carve out for yourself.

Your values, passions and vision are the driving force behind everything you do. You need to be clearly aware of each of these aspects, and understand exactly how they affect your actions and your personality, as they will define the other layers of perception.

Your passions: In the words of sales expert Brian Norris, "Passion is a gift of the spirit combined with the totality of all the experiences we've lived through. Passion is most evident when the mind, body and spirit work together to create, develop and articulate or make manifest our feelings, ideas and most sacred values". Most people will really only have three or four things that they are truly passionate about. These are likely to be the subjects that you cannot stop talking about and that light you up with an almost uncontrollable animation; they create within you an emotion and enthusiasm that is unquenchable. Your choice of how you spend your leisure time is a good indicator of the kinds of values and actions you might be passionate about. Passion is very difficult to fake, most people can spot insincerity when it comes to demonstrating one's passion.

Your values: (Your underlying belief systems.) These are the very foundations on which all your decisions are based, often unconsciously. The people you choose as friends, those whom you admire and respect, and those whom you dislike – each one of them reflects the values that you as an individual aspire to or disagree with. The types of jobs you accept are also a reflection of the values you hold.

Your vision: Every great leader has a vision, and quite often this can stem from a childhood experience. For example, Martin Luther King wanted a world where "…my four children will one day live in a nation where they will not be judged by the colour of their skin but by the content of their character…" He grew up in an America where racism and slavery were the norm, and his experience of these conditions caused him to see a vision that many did not understand at the time. Leaders will often have a vision that can cause controversy especially when others cannot see the value of that vision. However, it is important that you know what your vision is and where it is going to take you, because your vision is what will define the decisions you make, and the more aware of your vision you are, the more congruent your decision-making and your actions will be with the person you are; your authenticity will be complete.

When all of these pieces of the puzzle are connected to complete the picture, your inner identity will be in alignment with the individual perception you design. In time, as you evolve, your picture will continue to tell your story because the inner you rarely changes, except perhaps in degree or intensity.

Now, back to you and turning you into the leader you are going to become.

Transforming from good to great demands change. Great leaders are perceived to be congruent in whom they are and the message they communicate, both verbally and non-verbally. The gap analysis process that identity management does can help to map your current identity, assess your desired reality and identify conscious changes that will bridge the gap – taking you from where you are to where you want to be. Alignment through this process will sharpen your awareness of yourself, keep you in control of the reality you are presenting to others and trademark you as a great leader.

"When you bust apart the boxes that are limiting the success of your business – and access all of the potential in your organisation – you will increase profits."

Are barriers and silos interrupting the flow of results in your business? Accessing all areas of your company or your team allows you to tap into the true potential of the business. Sadly, some companies take a one-dimensional approach to their employees, putting them in boxes and making them operate in departmental silos, which limit their connections and their results. By applying some simple principles, leadership teams can create an 'access all areas' culture, and turn their companies into fully-functioning, flexible, change-proof entities that are ready to handle the challenges of today's business environment.

box busters boost businesses
HELEN MACDONALD

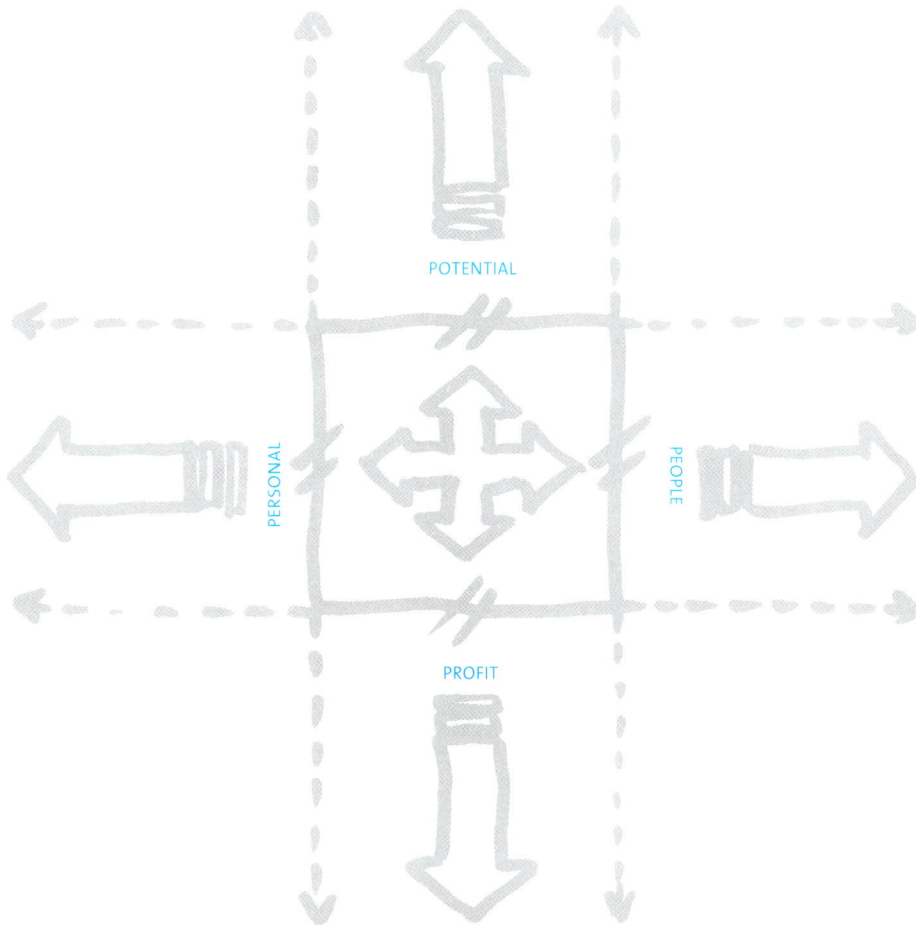

POTENTIAL

PERSONAL

PEOPLE

PROFIT

The usually enthusiastic business owner sitting opposite me sighed deeply. Following his first coaching session a month earlier, his homework had been to consciously look for blocks and under-performing areas or teams within his organisation. Now, as we started our second session, he had just finished telling me about the secret 'war' he had realised was being waged between two of his department managers. The two departments depended on one another for sales, customers and profits, yet they seemed to be determined to undermine each other as much as possible. Far from working together to create the best possible results, their staff made tasks as difficult for each other as they could and regularly set the other group up for failure.

My diagnosis was that this was a classic symptom of a 'boxed-in' business. The potential results of the whole company were being affected by the dysfunctional relationship between two groups of people that should have been working with each other – not against each other!

Further discussions revealed that the targets set for each department were actually encouraging this behaviour. Rather than pushing the two groups to work together toward common goals, they actually stood to achieve larger personal rewards if they ignored the needs of the other team.

LIMITING POSSIBILITIES

The problem with these behaviours is that they can severely limit the possible results of a company in four critical directions. In a 'boxed-in' business, individuals may believe that they are fully utilising their capacity, but in fact they are only functioning within the narrow confines of their own area of operation. Unaware of the invisible walls that surround them, they sometimes strive to do their best but are unable, or worse, unwilling to see beyond the boundaries.

People: Not fully connecting all the people in the various groups that can create positive results for the business can reduce customer satisfaction, diminish interpersonal relationships and lessen cross-departmental function. My client was experiencing this impact first-hand!

Personal: With so much emphasis at the moment on work/life balance, some people come to work with only part of themselves. In the worst-case scenario, they arrive with their bodies, leaving their hearts, minds and souls carefully stored at home! More often, they are not fully committed to the overall goals of the company and limit themselves to just looking after their own corner.

Potential: In a 'boxed-in' environment, the opportunity to maximise potential is limited. Individuals tend to do the minimum required to stay under the radar and not draw negative attention to themselves. By taking this approach they do not tap into all of their abilities, which limits their creativity and minimises their output.

Profit: At a bottom line level, all of these limitations have a negative effect on profit. By not creating an open-access culture, which can tap into all aspects of the individuals in the company, the penalty is paid in financial terms. As ex-Harvard professor David Maister proved in his 2001 study, the flow of profit comes from the development of a positive, open culture, not the other way around (*Practice What You Preach*, Free Press).

Perhaps your organisation's symptoms are not quite so severe. You may not have a silo situation and warfare may not have broken out, but you still need to keep a wary eye out for the damaging evidence of some of the more minor indicators of being 'boxed in'.

Are your people in a comfort zone? Do you ever get a sense that they are operating on autopilot? Do you find yourself being challenged by limitations that are set within the business, by narrow job definitions or by work-to-rule attitudes? Have you ever heard any of your team utter that dangerous phrase, "That's not my job"?

Are you still confident that you don't have a box infestation? If you are, that's great – and the even better news is that it is still possible to increase results in a box-free business by applying the box-busting principles.

MOVING YOUR TEAM FROM IMPEDING TO IMPROVING

In most businesses, individuals fall into one of three categories, the difference is in the number of people populating each category.

- The first, and most dangerous category is the **Impeders**. For a number of possible reasons, they regularly make mistakes and generally 'stuff things up'. They may have had bad work experiences in the past or picked up poor habits in previous jobs. They could be missing skills, knowledge or motivation.

With focused effort, close monitoring and the setting of realistic, small-step goals, these people can be reconnected with the business goals and become valuable team members. If these efforts fail, then they need to be helped to understand that different employment options would probably suit them better!

- In the second category are the **Imposters**. At first glance, they appear to be doing a good job. Look a little closer and you'll realise that they are actually really good at *looking* like they are doing a good job, rather than using their energy to *actually* do it! In some cases, they don't bring their true selves to the job. They turn up in the workplace with just a shadow of their full potential, not willing to commit to full participation. They often pretend to be involved in meetings or projects but miss deadlines or don't complete required tasks. Their goal is to do the minimum they can get away with, without drawing attention to themselves.

Often, the solution with imposters is as simple as letting them know that the game is up. Making them aware that their previous approach is no longer acceptable and setting clear expectations and consequences are two key elements for success in getting this group to perform at their best.

- The third group are the **Improvers**. In an ideal world, this is what you want everyone to be! These people are focused on getting the best possible results – that means they work on improving themselves, the systems they operate, and the relationships they have within the business and with their customers.

In simple terms, the key is to move the impeders in or out; encourage the imposters to truly turn up and tune up their performance; and make sure that you are recognising the efforts of your improvers.

BOX-BUSTING BENEFITS

Being a box-buster as a business owner, CEO or manager, can create major benefits for your business. By breaking down the barriers, you can access all of your business and all of your people – all of the time – which allows you to maximise the potential of your business and your team. In doing so, you will improve all of your business performance measures: communication, idea generation, creativity, productivity, and of course, the all-important bottom line – profit.

Creating, operating and maintaining a 'box-free' culture results in opportunities for breakthrough thinking. The answers to many of your business questions may exist within your teams – you just may never have asked the right person in the right way before!

So, how do we access all the positive benefits of a 'box-free' business?

> By breaking down the barriers, you can access all of your business and all of your people – all of the time – which allows you to maximise the potential of your business and your team.

It's a three-step process that begins with realising that there is an issue that is limiting the potential of the business. You want to find any silos, barriers or boxes that are operating within your company, and there are numerous ways to do this, ranging from the simple to the complicated. At the most complex are major culture surveys that gain input from all employees and analyse the results in detail. In the middle are straightforward business audits, and at the simplest end – you can just ask! Bring together a group of people from across the business and find out what they have seen happening. Using an external facilitator for this conversation and ensuring confidentiality of input can increase the effectiveness of this method.

So, step one is to find 'em, and step two is to bust 'em. Get some quick 'wins' on the board so your people can see that things are going to be different around here from now on. Start by setting cross-departmental targets that require teams to work together. Perhaps create small, cross-functional projects with outcomes that benefit all team members. Run some team events, anything from a Friday night social gathering to a more formal outcome-oriented experience.

My client decided to run some joint customer service training for his two warring departments, with an emphasis on managing internal client relationships. He also adjusted the two department managers' targets, so that each of their bonuses relied on the other group achieving its goals too.

Another of my clients decided on more extreme action: the managers were job-swapped! All of a sudden their bonuses were calculated based entirely on the performance of what used to be the 'opposition' department. They had to learn to deal with the pressures that faced the other part of the business, including handling the unreasonable demands of their old team. It very quickly brought home the need for them to work as an integrated team.

In other circumstances we have implemented communication cafés, management forums, job-sharing activities, interactive management meetings, and mentoring processes. All of these serve to bust apart the boxes in which people have comfortably put themselves and that are so often to the detriment of the business's results.

Step three is to keep 'em busted by making sure that your performance management, and reward and recognition systems continuously reinforce the importance of accessing the full potential of all employees. Using creative approaches, these can be very effective without eating up huge budgets.

MAINTAINING THE CHANGE – IT TAKES MORE THAN A QUICK FIX!

If you stretch a rubber band around a large object for a brief period of time, then take it off, it snaps back to its original size. People are like that, too. They think, 'here we go again with the latest management brain wave. If we just play along with it and wait a while, it'll all blow over and we can get back to normal!' We need to make sure that the changes become permanent.

Like the rubber band, to stretch a business or a team into a new shape requires long-term reinforcement of the new requirements. It cannot be done with a one-off fix. The individuals need to be crystal clear that this is not a temporary arrangement, but a new way of life!

Another element of this is to have clear and well-communicated goals that support the bigger picture of the vision and mission of the company. Recent studies have found that companies whose employees understand the mission and goals enjoy a 29 per cent greater return than other firms (Watson Wyatt Work Study 2005). However, in another survey, 75 per cent of respondents didn't think that their company's mission statement reflected the way the business really worked (Workplace 2000 Employee Insight Survey). Your mission statement needs to be more than just a framed parchment on the foyer wall!

Behaviour guidelines to sustain the core values of the business are also a positive force for change. With one client, we introduced clear behavioural requirements which successfully led to the voluntary resignation of a troublesome team member, without any other intervention. The remaining team had stronger morale and quickly improved their performance in a number of areas. This outcome required more than just the development, agreement and communication of the new behaviours. A key to successful maintenance of a 'box-free' culture is to have clear consequences for (as well as for not) continuing the open access approach. All the team members were clear about the rewards for following the guidelines, as well as the uncomfortable implications for breaking the agreements.

There are many solutions to the challenge of a 'boxed-in' business. All of them require a commitment from the leadership team to the eradication of this dangerous business practice.

To borrow from a classic line: To box or not to box, that is the question! And the answer is up to you. You can choose to take action, to become an active box-buster, or to put up with achieving less than the full potential of your business. *

"Give people what they want every time – and you'll always get what you want by default."

Most people have needs and wants and when they are satisfied, they move to a state of happiness; when you make people happy, they will happily reward you with what you want. In any negotiation, if you satisfy the needs and wants of the other party first, you will get what you want too. But in traditional negotiations, most people are only interested in what's in it for them and what they can get, so they end up butting heads with the other side, who is usually seeking that same goal. In any relationship, whether business or personal, ask yourself what will make the other party happy, and watch what happens when you oblige – often, it is more than you could ever have asked for or anticipated.

how to get what you want in any negotiation
RICK OTTON

TURNING OBJECTS INTO OPPORTUNITIES

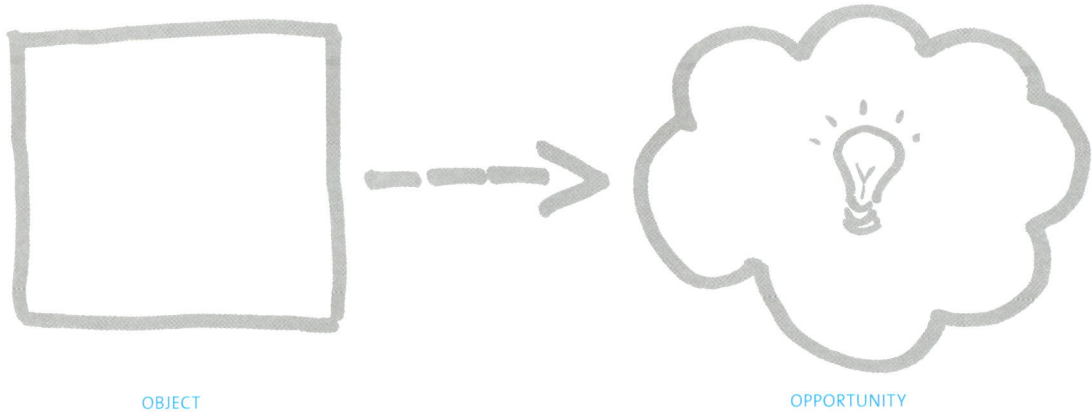

OBJECT

OPPORTUNITY

I have a friend who owns a shop in the USA that sells homemade chocolates. He recently told me that many of his customers are male, which is interesting as most chocolate consumers are female. What his customers have figured out is that if they keep their partners happy by treating them to delicious homemade chocolates, then they are able to get something that makes them happy in exchange, such as attending a football game or regular poker nights. Simply, by giving their partner something they want, in return they are getting what they want.

Why do people shop at 7-Eleven convenience stores? They don't sell their products at low prices or give buyers a lot of choice, what they do sell is convenience. They realised that if they gave people what they wanted they would also get what they wanted, which was brisk sales and huge profits. By giving people what they want, you too can get what you want every time.

Many company strikes would not occur if workers were unable to use their ability to withdraw their labour as a weapon to fight the company for more money. The company says it can't afford it and therefore the negotiation breaks down. But here is a secret – most people don't want more money, in fact surveys show that people rank 'higher pay' as only the third most important motivator when working for a company. Money in itself is only an object, and it carries with it no emotion, therefore of itself it cannot motivate people to do anything. It is the benefit or satisfaction that comes with the things money can provide that motivates people. So, if there is another way to provide people with the same benefit that the extra money would have afforded them, then the dispute can be resolved without the issue of money entering into it. For example, if a company asked an employee why they wanted the extra money they might find out that childcare, rather than more money, is the employee's real 'want'. The company that provides that service will keep their employees happy and everyone gets what they want.

In any conversation, whether it be personal or business, ask yourself what it is that the other person is saying, what do they really want? And, figure out a way to give it to them.

HOW TO USE OBJECT VERSUS OPPORTUNITY IN PROPERTY NEGOTIATIONS

In property negotiations, the process is traditionally a painful one in which no one achieves what they truly want. The head-butting often revolves around the sale price of the property; the vendor's goal is to achieve the highest possible price and the buyer wants to purchase at the lowest possible price. Yet, if you were to stop and ask the other party this simple question – what do you want? – you'd find that the answer is often not what you expect.

> In any conversation, whether it be personal or business, ask yourself what it is that the other person is saying, what do they really want? And, figure out a way to give it to them.

Objects have finite value; opportunity has infinite value. As an object, vacant land in the desert has a finite value. It is worth about the same as the parcel of land next door. Yet, if oil is discovered on that vacant land, the object suddenly becomes an opportunity for the landowner. And opportunity has infinite value.

When a vendor sells a property, it is not always about the price (object), it is sometimes simply about how easy the vendor can make it for the buyer to purchase the property (opportunity). If you can satisfy the needs and wants of the other party first, the contentious issue of price becomes secondary.

When buying a property, we should always ask the seller why they are selling and what their plans are for the future. It is often the case that people are not selling a property because they want to, but because they have to or because the money they will receive from the sale will enable them to obtain what they really want. Whatever the reason, quite often what they want is very different from what we might assume.

A pensioner might be selling a property because they can invest the funds from the sale to earn an income in retirement, so the sale of the property is all about filling their need for an income stream. Knowing this, you might agree to purchase the property by providing monthly payments in return for the seller financing you into the property. In this scenario, the seller receives a higher monthly income than they would if they cashed-out the property, which is what they really need. At the same time, as the buyer, you are provided with the funds to purchase the property directly from the seller.

How does object versus opportunity play out in this example? The house itself is the object, and if it is sold in a traditional transaction, it will remain as such. But, while having his or her own needs met, the seller can transform the house into an opportunity for the purchaser who will pay full price or more because their roadblocks to homeownership have been eliminated or reduced.

A common roadblock in these situations is the real estate agent's inability to communicate well with both parties involved in a property transaction. Sometimes the agent may not wish to tell you what the seller of the property is ultimately trying to obtain. As a result, many sellers get disgruntled when they sell a property and ultimately do not get what they were hoping to receive.

Objects can only be sold as opportunities when marketed that way, otherwise they remain objects and are given the same value as other objects. I own a property close to Sydney Harbour, with corresponding views. The value is the same as any other property of the same size, but what makes it a unique opportunity is its position. I use this property as a business retreat for American businesspeople. Now, from their perspective, what is the opportunity worth to spend time on

Sydney Harbour? They are willing to pay much more for the opportunity than they ever would if the property was simply matched up against another of the same size in a location that was not as interesting.

Consider this situation: A vendor, John, is selling a property for $355,000, which is market value, so that he can move interstate to care for a sick parent. The agent tells John that the property will not achieve market value in its present condition (based on a comparison with similar houses in the same suburb), but John can't afford to renovate the house.

While John is contemplating his situation, Paul and Mary come along looking to buy a property. They haven't yet saved quite enough money to cover the deposit and buying costs (stamp duty, legal expenses and so on). They are looking for a four-bedroom house, ideally with a pool, but they'd go without the pool for the right house. Paul and Mary earn enough to service the debt of $355,000, but they have some minor issues on their credit file (such as an unpaid mobile phone bill), which are making it difficult for them to get a bank loan. They answered a classified ad placed by John, simply because the headline read 'No Bank Qualifying', and they were curious.

John, Paul and Mary meet at the property. As they start talking, John learns that Paul and Mary do not have enough savings to cover the deposit and purchase costs, and he finds out about those minor credit issues that have prevented them from getting a bank loan in the past. John talks to them about the opportunity to own their own home; Paul and Mary love the property and are very excited about the possibility.

John does his due diligence on the buyers and vendor finances the property at the agreed price of $355,000. In lieu of not having a deposit, Paul and Mary agree to pay for cosmetic renovations, such as painting the interior and polishing the floorboards, prior to moving in.

Why does this arrangement benefit both the vendor and the buyer?

The vendor, John, is providing an opportunity for someone to move into their own home with no deposit. In return for providing the opportunity, he can achieve market value for the property by having Paul and Mary pay for the renovations. John will also receive an income stream from his vendor-financed property while he cares for his sick parent.

The opportunity for Paul and Mary is that they can buy this property with no deposit, and they can renovate it to match their tastes and preferences. They'll also capture the future capital gain as the property increases in value over time.

During this process, the vendor did not reduce the sale price of the property because he was offering financing (opportunity), and the buyers didn't negotiate for a lower sales price because they recognised they weren't just buying a house (object) they were receiving financing with the house (opportunity). Given the value of the opportunity, the issue of price becomes much less important in the eyes of the buyers.

In most situations, what people want is different to what they need. And while people will tell you what they want or desire, they will generally accept what they need. Paul and Mary desired a four-bedroom house with a pool, but they accepted John's house without a pool because the opportunity met their needs. By finding out what Paul and Mary needed, and making it possible for them, John was able to get what he wanted too.

HOW VENDOR FINANCING CAN TRANSFORM AN OBJECT INTO AN OPPORTUNITY

The process that John put in place is called vendor financing. It is when a seller assists a buyer to purchase the seller's property. While it's less common today, vendor financing has been around since the late 1800s in Australia and was once a very common way for vendors and buyers to transact property.

You can vendor finance in numerous ways: by financing a buyer's deposit; their legal costs and stamp duty; a percentage of the sales price; subsidising their interest rate; or funding renovations as John negotiated in our example. You can even provide the buyer with the entire purchase price of the property, making it easy for them to buy and therefore easy for you to sell. How well the vendor can match the needs and wants of the buyer will determine the price they can achieve and how quickly they can sell the property.

With vendor financing, you can see how an object with finite value (such as a house) transforms into an opportunity with infinite value when financing is attached.

"Our obsession with doing more and having more is corrupting our happiness; being happy is simply a matter of choice."

God, the Universe, your Higher Self – or whatever you call it – doesn't care what you do for a living. You might care, but God doesn't. What really matters is who you are being while you do whatever it is that you do. What God cares about is that you are happy. People want to be happy. We seek it endlessly through various forms of entertainment and leisure activities. Whenever I ask people what they really want, the most common answer is, "I want to be happy". So, what is happiness and how do you be happy?

god doesn't care what you do for a living
LORNA PATTEN

NEW PARADIGM – HAPPINESS NOW

when i BE happy
(loving, secure, at peace, content...)

i DO what i choose
(paint, write, start my own business, travel...)

and

i HAVE what i want
(enough money, time, energy...)

OLD PARADIGM – HAPPINESS LATER

when i HAVE what i want
(enough money, time, energy...)

then

i will DO what i choose
(paint, write, start my own business, travel...)

then

i will BE happy
(loving, secure, at peace, content...)

Being Happy Level 1 or *How to BE Who You Are While You Get On With Life.* In fact, you probably learnt (as most of us did) that happiness is mostly dependent on something outside of yourself. So you got on the treadmill of doing more/better/faster/quicker/higher/stronger so that you could prove you were good enough and earn enough approval/acceptance/validation/love to make you happy. It's a relentless cycle that will never deliver on its seductive promise of lasting happiness.

> Choosing to be happy is an inside job; it's a decision you can make no matter what your situation, circumstances, issues, problems or opportunities.

However, if you accept that happiness is a choice, and that you can choose it anytime, anywhere, no matter what's going on, then it doesn't matter what you have or what you do, and it doesn't matter what you think, feel or judge about what you have or do because you're happy. This simple paradigm shift opens the door to endless opportunities for personal growth and development, and allows you to experience true freedom – the freedom to be who you want to be in the world, to do what you really want to do, and to have all that you deserve and desire.

HAPPINESS IS A CHOICE

You can choose to be happy or choose to be unhappy. It's really that simple, and that's probably what makes it so difficult. You can make a choice to be happy now rather than waiting for whatever it is that you're waiting for to make you happy. What it takes is a willingness to change your mind and to shift your paradigm from an old way of thinking to a new one.

Choosing to be happy is an inside job; it's a decision you can make no matter what your situation, circumstances, issues, problems or opportunities. No matter what's going on in your life you can choose to be happy right now. But you probably won't, at least not in this moment.

The notion that you can choose to be happy, no matter what, flies in the face of all the evidence you have ever gathered that this is not so! Many people live life thinking, 'When I get this, or when I do that, then I'll be happy', and there are lots of people who are postponing their happiness for a date yet to be determined. But that day never comes.

BE HAPPY NOW

If you are striving to have everything just the way you want it before you decide to be happy – it's never going to work! It's the old carrot-and-stick routine and it isn't working any better now than it ever did. If you want a different outcome, you have to do something different, so flip the paradigm of have/do/be and see what happens when you be/do/have instead!

If you choose to be happy now and do what you desire, you'll have everything you ever really wanted. That's it. Be happy now. Simple.

Now, that doesn't mean that it's necessarily easy, or that you know how to be happy or how to choose to be happy. It's not something that was taught at school, at least I don't remember any classes on subjects such as

WHAT ARE YOU DOING?

Many people are obsessed with doing, doing, doing. They go hard – working hard, playing hard and filling every available minute with activity. If they are not doing something, they think they are wasting time or missing out. Some people find it almost impossible to sit still for more than a few minutes, fuelled by a restless energy to keep going, doing, achieving and moving. And the reason this is happening is because people want to feel good, they want to be happy and they think if they just do more, have more, get further, achieve more…then they'll be happy.

OLD PARADIGM: DO MORE AND HAVE LOTS AND ONE-DAY-SOMEDAY-BE-HAPPY

If you think your happiness is dependent on what you have and what you do, you're bound to spend a lot of time doing more and having lots – and feeling anxious at least some of the time. You may feel happy when what you have and do is judged to be 'good' or 'right' by yourself and others. And you may feel unhappy when what you have and do is judged to be 'not good enough', 'bad' or 'wrong' by yourself and others.

This happens because you have confused the intrinsic value of who you really are with the relative value of what you have and do. You have done this by judging the relative worth of what you have and do (compared to what you think it should be and/or what others have said it should be) and attaching that value judgement to yourself, as if it is the truth about you as a person.

For example, when someone says to you, "Good job" you probably feel good. That's because you have decided that the other person's value judgement of 'good' means that you are good (or okay, worthwhile and so on). But as soon as someone says to you, "That was a lousy job" the pattern kicks in again and you feel bad.

When you believe that your happiness is a direct result of how you and others judge what you have or do, then you are bound to experience momentary happiness when you gain approval or validation from yourself or others. Conversely, you are bound to experience varying degrees of dissatisfaction or unhappiness anytime you or others do not approve of or validate what you have or do.

When you or others judge what you do as being 'not good enough' or 'wrong' you probably have a tendency to take it personally, which means that you interpret that value judgement as a personal attack, and decide that it means you are 'not good enough'. Then you begin to feel a mixture of feelings and emotions such as hurt, shame, guilt, anger and despair.

Agreeing with the relative value judgements you place on yourself (or the ones that you perceive come from others) guarantees that you will only have sporadic and fleeting experiences of real happiness. And it often leads to an endless quest to get better at doing things (and thus to be better and feel better about yourself). This is not the path to happiness now, it's the path to one-day-someday-happiness – maybe.

WHO ARE YOU BEING?

The answer to this question is the key to your happiness. And it has nothing – absolutely nothing – to do with what you do or don't do. It has to do with who you are being now and who you choose to be in the next moment. You'll find the answer inside yourself, in what you know about yourself, who you dream of being and what you desire to experience and express.

NEW PARADIGM: BE HAPPY NOW, DO WHAT I CHOOSE AND HAVE WHAT I WANT

Maybe you have already begun to realise that just doing more, better, harder, faster isn't giving you what you really want. Maybe you are not as happy, fulfilled and at peace as you expected to be after all you've done and achieved. And maybe you have begun to question how much longer you are going to wait to be happy and live the life you dream.

You can choose to be happy right now. It doesn't mean that you have to love everything that's going on in your life. And it doesn't mean that you'll just sit down in a corner and stop caring about what happens. It simply means that you can choose to be, and to express yourself in any way you want – open, honest, loving, kind, generous, compassionate, confident, joyful, aware, powerful, abundant, caring, trusting and so on. The possibilities are only limited by your imagination.

Each of us has a unique gift to give the world and we give that gift most fully when we remember the truth about who we are and what we are really here for. Who you are is magnificent, loving, creative and powerful. And what you are really here to do is become all that you are and to be the most magnificent you that you can become.

You are not here to do anything in particular. You are here to fulfil the promise of your own magnificence – however you choose to express it. When people are happy they make more resourceful choices, and are more productive and fulfilled. When you feel a strong pull to a particular vocation or when you feel a deep urge to do something, listen to yourself and follow what you know is right for you. This is the path of least resistance, the path of fulfilment. When you embark on a path of conscious intention to be who you really are, no matter what you are doing, then everything you do will truly reflect the joy of being who you are.

When you make the distinction that who you are is not what you do, that the relative value and worth of what you do is not the same as your self-value, then you are free to do anything you choose, anything that makes your heart sing. When you accept your intrinsic value and worth – the fact that you are you, and that the gift you are here to give is the gift of simply being you – then it's pretty simple to choose to be happy.

"Every customer is a niche market of one; if you're not niche marketing, you're missing the point."

Search wide and dig deep – most businesses make the mistake of trying to reach too many people in their market, which leads to increased competition, soaring promotional costs and minimal differentiation. Smart marketers take the opposite approach; the smaller your market, the better suited your products and services will be for that market – which ultimately means that you can raise your prices, increase your profits and virtually eliminate your competition.

niche guys finish first
GIHAN PERERA

NICHE MARKET

MASS MARKET

success is that he's chosen a tiny niche market. He's not teaching your *bird* how to talk; he's not teaching you how to look after your parrot; and he's not going for the wider market of pet owners. Rather, he's chosen a very specific group of people. And while there may not be many of them, his e-book is perfect for them.

The more tightly you define your market, the easier it is to create a product or service that precisely matches what they want.

My own web design company, First Step Communications, is another example of niche marketing. Since 1997, we have been working with 'information experts' – professional speakers, trainers, consultants, coaches and authors – to develop their websites and online strategies. As a result of specialising in this particular niche market, the company has gained a number of competitive advantages:

- Because our website products are tailored to the needs of this market they are more valuable to clients.
- We understand our clients' industry, so they don't have to waste hours explaining to us how their business works.
- We speak their language, which puts us a long way ahead of competitor web design companies.
- Clients see us more as a consultant than a supplier. They ask for assistance and trust our advice – even when we advise them about choosing a supplier!
- I have been invited to speak at industry conferences in Australia, New Zealand, South Africa, Canada and the UK. By contrast, most other suppliers have to pay for sponsorship and trade show booths at industry conferences.
- We consistently get referral work from clients who recommend us to their colleagues in the same industry.

WHY NICHE?

Niche marketing delivers many competitive benefits. In addition to those that we've already discussed, your business can benefit from:

Higher prices: A brain surgeon can charge more than a GP because of her specialisation. Through niche marketing you can charge a higher price for your products and services because they more closely match the customer's requirements.

Most businesses make the mistake of casting their marketing nets too wide, scared that if they don't reach out to everyone they will miss opportunities and lose market share to their competitors. But in fact, the more tightly you define your market, the easier it is to create a product or service that precisely matches what they want. Conversely, the wider your market, the more generic you have to make your product so that it is more appealing and applicable to everyone. Casting the marketing net too widely is why small online bookshops go broke trying to compete with Amazon.com; why small retailers go out of business when a large department store opens up nearby; and why motivational speakers with a generic 'one size fits all' speech suffer when the conference industry takes a downturn.

By all means search wide to find the right niche markets, and when you do, dig deep. In this chapter, I'll explain why niche marketing works, how to identify what makes a good niche, and show you how to make the most of one when you find it.

WHAT IS A NICHE MARKET?

Broadly speaking, a niche market is simply a clearly defined segment of a larger market. To illustrate, here are some examples of businesses catering to niche markets:

- A sales trainer with a focus on a particular industry, such as pharmaceutical companies or financial planners.
- A bookshop owner who caters for readers who want to create, run or join book clubs.
- A financial planner who concentrates on a particular demographic group, such as young professionals or single parents.

One of my favourite niche marketing stories is about internet marketing expert Frank Kern, who makes $1,500 a month from a website selling an e-book that teaches people how to get their parrots to talk. The key to his

Less competition: When you go head-to-head with Amazon.com, you'll probably lose. But if your focus is on local book clubs interested in theme nights, you'll be targeting needs that Amazon.com doesn't service.

Lower advertising costs: Instead of aiming for expensive mass-media advertising, you can focus on highly targeted exposure that is more suited to your market – such as industry magazines, local newspapers, pay-per-click internet advertising, and sponsorship of specific events.

Greater depth: You'll learn more about your clients and their problems, which makes it easier for you to provide suitable solutions.

Easier sales process: When your clients know that you're offering specific solutions for their real problems, it makes the sales process so much easier for you.

Perceived expertise: You'll become recognised as an expert in the niche, rather than a supplier pushing a product or service to the market.

Keep in mind that every customer is already a niche market of one, with their own fears, desires, goals and ideas. The more closely you match your product or service to that one customer's needs, the more likely they will be to buy. If you're not already doing niche marketing, you're missing the point.

SO WHAT'S STOPPING YOU?

If niche marketing is such a wonderful concept, why aren't more businesses doing it? Why is there so much sameness in the market, with every supplier offering the same as everyone else?

Our biggest fear is that by aiming at a specific niche we're immediately closing off every other segment of the market. In other words, we're afraid that we'll become so specialised that we can't cater to any other market segment.

This is more perception than reality. While specialisation certainly makes you more attractive to a particular niche, it doesn't necessarily make you any less attractive to anyone else. The only people who care about your chosen niche market are the people in that market segment, and they'll love the fact that you're catering for them more closely. No one else cares! Frank (the parrot guy) has a number of other websites – none of which relate to parrots! The parrot owners love his parrot

talking e-book, and his other niche markets love the e-books that relate to them.

Remember too that choosing to specialise in a particular niche market doesn't necessarily mean that you have to exclude other market segments. Just because you create a new business card to cater specifically for your niche market doesn't mean that you have to burn your old cards! Keep working with your existing market for as long as you like; although I suspect that you'll soon find your niche market will rapidly become more profitable.

WHAT MAKES A SUCCESSFUL NICHE?

A good niche market has three characteristics: it must be identifiable, feasible and profitable. In other words, you must be able to find it, reach it and sell to it. Let's look at each of these three characteristics in turn.

Identifiable: The internet has made it much easier to find good niche markets. However, rather than seeking out new and unfamiliar markets, look at your own business first. You'll find that the best niche markets for your business already exist within your customer base, and because you already know something about them, it makes sense to start there. Look through your customer base and see if you can categorise groups of customers according to any of these criteria:

- *Demographic (Who are they?):* Do you deal mainly with men? Women? People of a certain age group? A particular ethnic group? In particular industries? At certain income levels?
- *Geographic (Where are they?):* Are they from particular countries? Certain local areas? Clustered around certain cities?
- *Psychographic (Why do they buy?):* Are they facing similar problems? Do they have similar goals? Are their businesses at similar stages?

If you haven't done this exercise before, you might be surprised to find that you've already got some strong niche markets among your current customers. Imagine what could happen if you started catering for their specific requirements. Next, extend this analysis to your wider market. After all, your customer base might not be representative of the market as a whole.

Feasible: Simply put, can you reach this niche market easily? If not, it's probably not worth pursuing it. For example, if you sell golf clubs, you might discover a small pocket of left-handed customers who have bought putters from you. That's a clearly identifiable niche market, but can you reach them easily? In the past it might have been a challenge to target that particular group, but today, with internet tools such as Google's pay-per-click advertising, it's now easier to target identifiable groups such as this than ever before.

When considering whether your market is feasible, ask yourself whether they tend to congregate in the same area – whether it's an industry association, an online chat room, a church group or reading the same newspaper. If they do, it'll be easier to reach them. For example, in the health sector, it's easier to target people with a chronic ailment such as snoring, than it is to target those with a more general but transient ailment, such as the common cold. That's because people with an interest in a specific topic area (in this case, snoring) will be attracted to certain websites, chat rooms and groups, whereas people with a more general interest (those with a common cold) will not be directed to such specifically identifiable locations and therefore will be much more difficult to locate.

Profitable: Once you've identified a potential market niche, ask yourself three questions to help determine how profitable it might be:

1. Do they have money?
2. Are they willing to pay?
3. Will they pay enough?

These are related but different questions. For example, teenagers have money and are willing to pay for clothes, music, mobile phone ring tones and jewellery, but if you're trying to sell them a self-help book to boost their self-esteem, you're likely to face an uphill battle getting them to spend! Similarly, if you're selling golfing lessons to consumers, you might find that they do have money and are willing to pay, but there's an upper limit to what they will pay because learning golf is a leisure activity and they compare the cost of that to the cost of other leisure activities. (As an aside, if you repackage your golfing lessons to focus on golf as an essential networking tool for company executives, you can conduct entire golfing retreats for corporate clients. It's a smaller, but more profitable niche.)

HOW DO YOU FOCUS ON THE NICHE?

When you find an identifiable, feasible and profitable niche, it's time to roll up your sleeves and start working with that market. The exact activity will vary, depending on your business and your market. However, these are some general issues to consider:

Marketing collateral: Modify your business cards, brochures, website content, email templates and other marketing materials to focus on that specific niche.

Industry knowledge: Immerse yourself in that market – subscribe to their magazines, attend their conferences, join their associations, and so on.

Strategic communication: Design and deliver specific communication pieces – newsletters, email broadcasts, and so on – for this niche, so that they see your new positioning.

Tailored solutions: Examine your products and services, and adapt them for this niche market. Some will require only minor changes, others will require extensive revisions – and you might even have to create some entirely new products.

Most importantly, start thinking of yourself as an *expert consultant* to that niche market. Ask yourself, if you were the world's leading expert in this area, what would you know? What would you say? How would you communicate with people in that market? What would you read? What would you write? Then act as if you are that expert. This is not about faking it or deceiving your clients, it's about establishing your expert attitude and mind-set when dealing with them.

NICHE MARKETING WORKS – AND NICHE GUYS REALLY DO FINISH FIRST

Niche marketing works – it sets you apart from your competitors; gives you closer and more trusted access to your clients; allows you to create joint ventures with other businesses to serve the same clients better; and simplifies your business systems and processes.

Some business owners worry that when they choose a niche market, they will eventually get all the business they can out of that niche and be left with nothing else to sell. While that is a possibility, in most cases people tend to underestimate rather than overestimate the potential of a well-chosen niche market. When you've got the right niche, and you become the recognised expert in that niche, the sky's your limit. ✐

"Systems allow us to work efficiently, expending less time and energy, and that means that they can improve our quality of life and profitability."

Most people hate systems. They believe they are limiting, solid and rigid. But the reality is that systems are flexible and exist to serve us. It's just that we sometimes get it around the wrong way and believe that we are there to serve the systems, which creates frustration and fear. Getting it right is easy when you understand the balance and relationship between systems and how we use them.

systems are the answer
SHARONNE PHILLIPS

THE SYSTEMS MODEL™

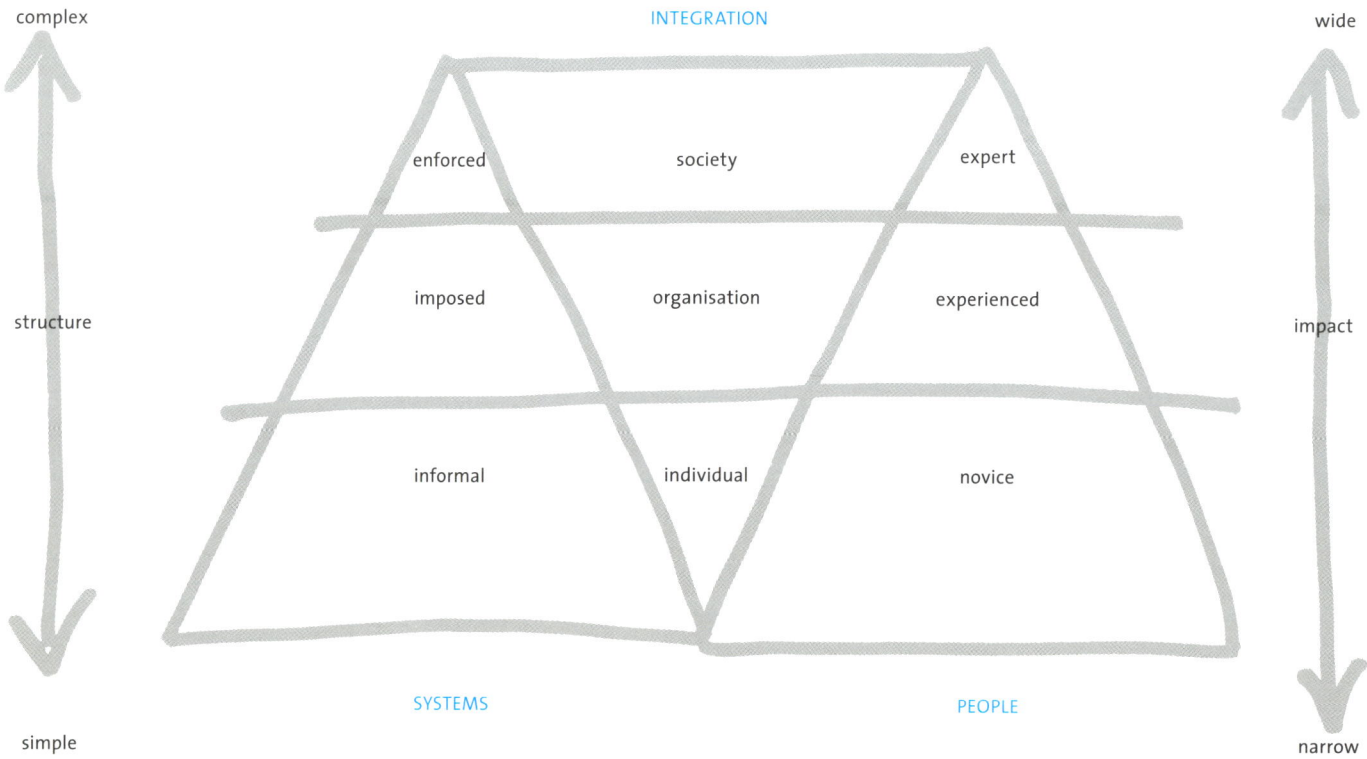

complex

INTEGRATION

wide

enforced   society   expert

structure

imposed   organisation   experienced

impact

informal   individual   novice

SYSTEMS

PEOPLE

simple

narrow

There are three main components to systems:

1. the systems themselves
2. the people who use them, and
3. the integration between the two.

It is important to understand each of these components in order to be able to harness the energy and power of each, and to bring out the best in everyone. This is when businesses fire up and perform brilliantly, and when relationships can truly hum with harmony.

First, let's consider what makes people tick. Obviously there are many different things, but I want to focus on the attitudes and experiences people have in relation to their work and the things they do in their working lives. For this purpose we can categorise people into three main groups: novices, experienced and experts.

- **Novices** are the people who perform particular tasks, it might be working on a factory process line, doing data entry in an office, or checking and writing emails and reports. The novice might have well-developed skills and expertise in their area of work, but they lack autonomy and authority when completing their tasks. They often have a general knowledge about things, but are not asked for the information that they can share.

- **Experienced** people know a lot about a smaller range of things. They often work at middle management levels and might supervise other staff. They have a level of autonomy over their work and might be asked their opinion about what products or processes work, or which software application would suit a particular purpose. They liaise between senior management and the staff that complete the bulk of the general work in the organisation.

- **Experts** have detailed and precise knowledge about a specialised area. They tend to tell other people what to do, and are often the major decision maker in an organisation. They have a great deal of influence in their workplace, regardless of the level at which they work. Experts are often well educated, and have a great deal of proficiency in their chosen field.

It is important to understand each of these components in order to be able to harness the energy and power of each, and to bring out the best in everyone. This is when businesses fire up and perform brilliantly, and when relationships can truly hum with harmony.

Systems can also be described in three main groups: informal, imposed and enforced. They each have their specific purpose and application, and each type of person prefers, or has a natural aptitude for, one type of system.

- **Informal** systems are the most flexible and adaptable. These are the systems that are created 'on the fly' and are easy to change depending on the conditions. For example, we might change the system that we use to travel to work depending on the weather, or the tasks we have to complete on any given day. These systems are so flexible that we often don't even recognise them as systems. They allow us to plan what we need to do, and give us some structure around it so that our actions and implementation are more streamlined and efficient.

- **Imposed** systems are those that provide a higher level of structure, with some flexibility. There might appear to be limited choice in these systems, but in fact there is a degree of choice in selecting and implementing them. In general, people need to learn how to use these systems, for example a software application that is supplied with a computer, or that is used by a particular department in an organisation. These systems can be removed or configured to suit the user (that is, they can be flexible), but it is often easier or cheaper to use them as they are supplied.

- **Enforced** systems are the most complex of systems; our laws and regulations are examples of enforced systems. There is often a punitive component associated with their use, so that if the user does not comply with the system they might be fined or even sentenced to gaol. In general, enforced systems are developed for the common good, they reflect the moral, ethical, financial and perhaps religious ideals of a society. Enforced systems have to be explained to the users so that they can make sense of them and comply with them (as is done through the advertising campaigns that accompany changes in our tax or industrial relations laws, for example).

Different systems serve different purposes. The informal systems tend to serve the needs of individuals, imposed systems tend to serve the needs of a community or organisation, and enforced systems tend to serve a much larger group of people, such as a social system and national or international groups.

It is easiest for people to use the type of system that best suits the required purpose, and that matches their individual preference. For example, a novice is most comfortable using informal systems that serve the individual, an experienced person likes imposed systems that serve a community or organisation, and an expert has a natural affinity with enforced systems that serve a society, particularly if that enforced system is within their field of expertise. In fact, at each level, each type of person is often involved in developing, creating and using the systems at their preferred level.

There is a constant flux between the levels of systems and the way we behave around them or use them. We might be novices as we do some things, but experienced or expert when completing other tasks. Our comfort and ability to use the different systems will change with our level. Sometimes others determine our level based on how they see us and our influence and autonomy, rather than our actual abilities.

It is possible for a person to move up or down one level, but it is much harder to cross two levels – this is when systems stop making sense. The novice does not like or understand formal, complex, enforced systems (they must be explained to them), and the expert does not value the informal systems that the novice uses, even though these might be the most relevant for task completion. The expert has the greatest understanding and respect for enforced systems, whereas the novice finds them too complicated and alien to be of much use in their daily dealings.

PRACTICAL APPLICATIONS OF THE SYSTEMS MODEL™

Micro and small business owners have a great deal of difficulty if they cannot move between the different levels. They must operate at the novice level using informal systems as they go about 'getting business done' every day. They must use imposed systems, such as their computer applications, accounting systems, supply and invoicing systems. And they must use and be aware of the enforced systems that are necessary for them to comply with business practices – such as tax and liability laws, insurances, registrations and professional requirements. If the business owner gets trapped into focusing only on doing what they know how to do, they can be caught in the cycle of micro-managing their business and projects – and this can prevent the business from growing.

If a small business owner expands their business and requires staff, they must employ the staff using the mind-set that is appropriate to the level equal to or above that which they are recruiting for. For example, if the business owner decides to employ a personal assistant, they must do so from the mind-set of an experienced person (or an expert) employing an experienced person. If they employ from the position and focus of a novice, they are likely to get a novice (you cannot employ 'above' your level unless you are thinking from that level) when they really need an experienced (or even expert) personal assistant. In this case, the person applying for the job will not have the required experience (as they too will be at the novice level). So the good intentions and need to employ good staff to assist in the growth of the business will not be realised. This pattern can explain poor recruitment practices and is often expressed in high levels of staff turnover that can adversely affect profits, efficiency, business growth and development, and job satisfaction.

It is important to get the match between people, the system that they use and the purpose of that system correct in order to maximise the efficiency, work satisfaction and profitability of any business. ✏

"Some people just seem to be able to draw money toward them – I call these people money magnets."

Let's say you took all the money in the world and gave an equal share to everyone – I can guarantee you that in less then five years you would find the money grouped again in the hands of only a few people. Why would this happen? Is it simply a matter of luck? No. It is because these people are what I call money magnets. The secrets to creating and powering your money magnet are within you.

become a money magnet
HELEN SHAO

UNLEASH YOUR HIDDEN POWER

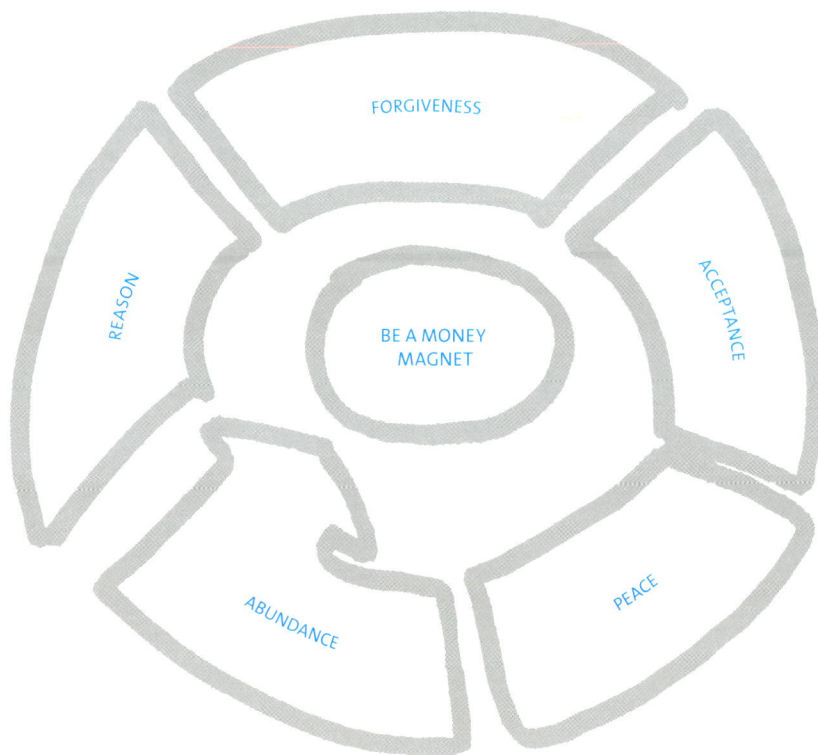

FORGIVENESS

REASON

ACCEPTANCE

BE A MONEY MAGNET

ABUNDANCE

PEACE

WHAT IS STOPPING YOU FROM BECOMING A MONEY MAGNET?

We all have issues to deal with that act as roadblocks or barriers to our becoming money magnets. These could come in the form of the attitudes we inherit from our families, our deep-seated fears and anxieties, or maybe even from the pressures and stresses of modern life.

Some of the attitudes or beliefs that commonly hold people back from becoming money magnets may sound familiar to you:

Money is the root of all evil.

Honest people don't make real money.

You have to be born lucky to make any money in this world.

And some of the excuses that stop people from being able to attract money into their lives might even be ones you've used yourself:

It's okay for everyone else to be rich, but not me.

If I just work hard at my job I will get rich.

I am worried that I am going to fail.

The list goes on and on. The important thing is to recognise that we all have certain beliefs and values attached to money, and if they are negative rather than positive they can be the roadblocks that prevent us from becoming money magnets. So, how can we overcome them?

HOW DO YOU CREATE YOUR MONEY MAGNET?

I want to show you:

- how to discover the secrets of wealth in your subconscious mind
- how to manifest abundance, and
- how good it feels to be free from fear and pain about money.

Abundance means many different things to different people. For some people it means having their needs met – having no fear of being homeless or hungry. For others, it is about dedicating their lives to the single-minded pursuit of excellence in their chosen field. And for others, it means acquiring the kind of wealth that gives them the opportunity to live a comfortable life or to be able to pass on that financial security to their children. Whatever it means to you, it is personal.

Of all the things we learn about money, most of us never learn about the energy of money. Most of us are not taught the principles of manifesting abundance, or how to create powerful, motivating beliefs, or how to visualise the success we desire until our subconscious accepts it as being real. And we never discover how it is possible to create wealth almost effortlessly. Instead, most of us believe what we are told about working hard, that nothing comes easily, that life is hard, and that money doesn't buy happiness.

I want to share with you the secret that helped me to attract money into my life.

THE KEY SECRET TO ATTRACTING MONEY

Let me tell you something about my life. I was born in China in 1961, which was a year of terrible economic depression and natural disaster. At this time, there was intense rivalry between China and the Soviet Union. In the push to industrialise China, the normal production of food was disrupted, crops failed and many people found themselves literally starving to death. My school was officially closed after Chairmen Mao ordered all school students to relocate to the countryside and learn from farm peasants and simple workers. My parents were not communists and were taken to a camp for re-education.

Without anyone to look after me, my mother locked me in the house and forbade me to leave. She told me that our family was now outcast. Both my parents realised that there were great dangers should I stray outside our home, but being a child, I didn't believe their warnings and escaped to play with some of my friends outside. One afternoon, after I had met up with these 'friends' outside my home, I was set upon as a traitor to the communist way. Apparently their parents had told them that I was unfit for the company of 'good' kids. I was now a pariah. I was spat on and bruised after a number of them hurled rocks straight into my disbelieving face. I fled and they gave chase, pursuing me all the way to our school library. The librarian was an old man who knew my mother. He took one look at my crying face before realising my predicament. He sent my tormentors away with a few simple questions that made these other children regret their cruel behaviour.

I later found out that the old man was a Qigong master. It was my first experience with the power of Qigong. For two years, almost every day, I visited the elderly librarian, and he taught me many things about life and showed me the secret of how to achieve anything you want in life.

I remember once being asked by our art teacher to draw a teacup for homework. After spending the entire afternoon on my drawing I showed it to my mother, she looked at it and said, "That is not looking good, I think you should do more drawing instead of going out to play". She went on to say that I should not try to finish my homework in a hurry – she suggested that I should draw at least five or more and then hand them in. I told my mother that she hadn't seen the other 50 drawings before this one! I continued and did another 50 drawings which I handed in the next day, even so, I still only got a 'B'. I went to ask my Qigong master why I was not good at drawing. He said to me, "You can't be good at everything, but the key secret of getting what you want, when you want it, is to enhance and improve what you do the best, then you can be the champion".

THE FORMULA FOR ATTRACTING MONEY

Over time, the elderly librarian showed me the secret world of Qigong. Afterwards, I practised these techniques to master my own destiny and today I use them to help others to master their destinies.

In Chinese, 'Qi' means air, and represents energy and life. 'Gong' means technique. Qigong is a breathing technique. 'Jing' means quietness, and Jing-gong is the combination of Western meditation and Eastern breathing technique. Using Jing-gong, people can uncover their subconscious mind, discover their value system and master their own destiny. The goal of Qigong is to enhance the quality of people's lives. By doing Qigong people can learn the way to open their energy channels and maintain balance.

"Why is it so important to get into the silence and stillness?" I asked my Qigong master one day. "Because silence is one of the elements of attracting wealth, happiness and spiritual wealth," my Qigong master replied. "There is a formula that will help you to smash through those roadblocks that stop you achieving what you desire most in life, it is:

S + S + S = Wealth, Health and Happiness

I practised these techniques to master my own destiny and today I use them to help others to master their destinies.

The first 'S' stands for Silence, the second for Stillness and the third for Solitude." My Qigong master continued, "Through quietness and silence we can uncover our most powerful mind. Some say we only used 10 per cent of our minds, others say we only use two per cent. There is so much that we don't know about how powerful the human mind can really be".

Research into psychology and studies of world leaders, scientists, musicians, physicists, industrialists, inventors and other famous people proves that silence and stillness is one of the great formulas many have used, whether unwittingly or intentionally, since the beginning of time.

It is this formula that helped me to go through the toughest times in life. After escaping from China I arrived in Australia in 1989 with US$40 in my pocket, a little English and a determination to succeed in my new adopted country.

I used Qigong and meditation to keep me focused on what I wanted in life. I won a scholarship from the Australian National University in Canberra to study my PhD in applied finance, and purchased my first home within 100 weeks of arriving in Australia. I have achieved my financial independence by applying this formula again and again. I believe we are all the masters of our own destiny and that we have the power to attract the wealth and happiness we deserve.

I remember my Qigong master telling me the Buddhist story about human power: the gods were trying to think of a suitable hiding place for mind power so that mankind would not have the benefit of this great omnipotence. One god suggested hiding it on the top of the highest mountain, but another argued that sooner or later man would conquer even the highest mountain and find it. Another god suggested they hide it in the sea; he too was overruled by another saying that man would conquer the depths and eventually find it. Yet another god put forward the idea of burying it deep underground, but like all the other suggestions this was overruled; as one god pointed out, man would excavate the earth. One wise old god, hearing the argument, put forward the motion that human power should be hidden within the human mind, for, as he pointed out, Man would never think of looking there. The motion was carried.

THE 70-DAY JOURNEY TO ATTRACTING MONEY

The journey involves lessons in reason, forgiveness, acceptance, peace and happiness, love and joy. During the journey we discover why we are here, we learn to forgive ourselves, we learn to accept who and what we are, and we get to the stage of being at peace.

- **Stage 1**: We discover the reasons why we are here. Knowing these reasons gives us powers to achieve whatever it is that we want. During this stage we identify why we should love ourselves and why we deserve to have lots of money. We learn to manifest these reasons and install them into our subconscious minds by using Jing-gong techniques.
- **Stage 2**: We find ways to forgive ourselves. During this stage we identify 20 things that we have either done or not done that were wrong, and that we need to forgive ourselves for.
- **Stage 3**: We install acceptance into our subconscious minds and learn to accept who we are. During this stage we learn to manifest self-acceptance through statements such as: "I accept that I am a lovely mother to my son, and a lovely daughter to my parents".
- **Stage 4**: During this stage we learn to be at peace. We manifest peace into the subconscious by using the words: "I am at peace within myself, I can't hear any noise. I don't feel any negativity around me. I am at peace".
- **Stage 5**: In the final stage we learn to be happy and to attract money. This is achieved by applying the silence + stillness + solitude formula. During this stage we identify 100 items that we want to spend money on in the near future, and the amount of money required for those things – this is the sum of money that you will learn to attract.

This journey has changed lots of people's lives, including my own, and I hope that it will change yours too.

"People are becoming numb. It is that sense of being constantly overloaded – and it's costing businesses millions of dollars every day."

Have you ever felt like you are living – but not really alive? In the past we had clear lines of communication and clear boundaries around what was expected of us – at home and at work. Today, we have so many sources of information and communication bombarding us that we are becoming overloaded, and mentally shutting down. This numbing is costing businesses millions of dollars in performance and it is also leading to people feeling a sense of disconnection with themselves and others.

numb
SCOTT STEIN

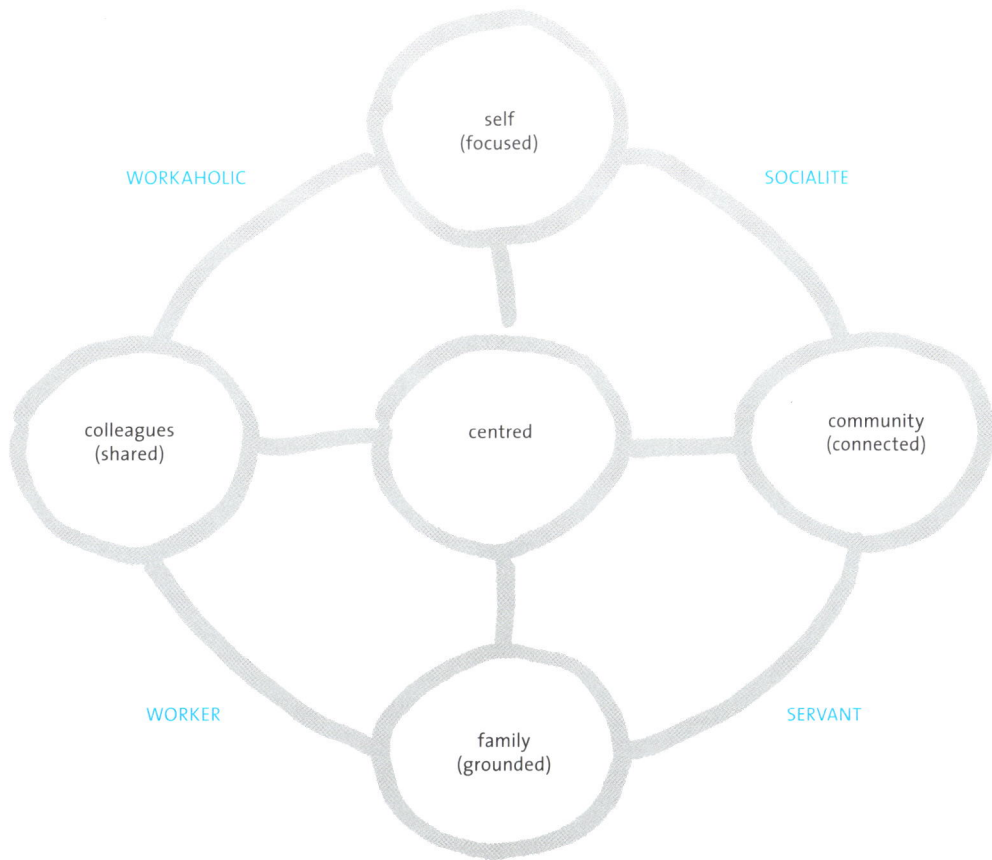

THE NUMBING OF OUR WORKING LIVES: LOSING TRACK OF WHAT IS IMPORTANT

The nature of work has changed significantly over the past 20 years. We have shifted from being a workforce of committed, long-term employees to living in an ever-changing business environment focused on short-term tasks that encourages people to operate on autopilot and independently of the community around them.

> As we've increased the amount of time and energy spent at work, it has reduced the active leisure time available for us to relax, be with our families and reconnect with our individual needs.

In speaking with many CEOs and senior managers, the common challenge that they are facing is not business infrastructure, systems or assets – but how to get their people off autopilot and beginning to really think again. With the numbing of the workforce people are showing up to work overwhelmed and unconsciously limiting their creative capabilities.

One of the drivers for this numbing is the increase in the reliance on technology and the daily information overload. We now have communication that bombards staff 24 hours a day, seven days a week. The challenge is not getting information, it is in skilling people to be able to synthesise the information they receive and to be able to sift the misinformation from the valuable information.

The internet was designed to enable people to be connected, but in reality it has resulted in many people feeling disconnected, and losing a sense of community. We can communicate continuously via email and never really say anything. Email communications have largely replaced the spoken word, we email each other rather than picking up the phone or going to see someone. And one of the great dangers of email communications is the opportunity for miscommunication, which in itself can occupy hours of people's time as they unravel the unintended offence that has been caused by a poor choice of words, an imagined 'tone of voice' or an inability to get the right point across in writing. The mere existence and use of these technological tools is no longer a business advantage – real advantage will be gained by the organisations that learn how to harness and manage their use so that they work for the organisation rather than simply causing unnecessary

THE NUMBING OF OUR PERSONAL LIVES: BEING CENTRED VERSUS OVERCOMMITTED

If you ask anyone to describe what is different about our society and how we live today compared to 20 years ago, you will get a range of different responses, but underlying these will be some common themes that are the cause of numbing. One of the key themes is our inability to get reconnected with our centre and be truly content with our lives. We are now more consciously aware of the need to reconnect with our selves at a mental, physical and spiritual level, and to balance this with time spent with our families. But as we've increased the amount of time and energy spent at work, it has reduced the active leisure time available for us to relax, be with our families and reconnect with our individual needs. The results of this are seen in the splintering of families and skyrocketing divorce rates. And it leads to common behavioural patterns that we will examine later in this chapter.

ARE YOU LIVING NUMB?

- The time you have with your spouse or kids is spent in between trying to cram in other things, usually related to work.
- You feel that you never have the chance to fully recharge your batteries – if only you could get a couple of days to yourself you would be back to 100 per cent.
- When you reflect on your life you realise that you have spent time being numb – just going through the motions.
- You can't remember the last time you really laughed with your family.

If you can relate to more than a couple of these points, you are living in the numb zone.

activity. Those with the ability to connect to the community outside their organisations will also create business relationships that move quicker than the traditional business, in real time.

ARE YOU WORKING NUMB?

- You read through your inbox or listen to your voicemail, but half an hour later you can't remember what the messages said or who they were from because there were so many.
- You have woken up in the middle of the night realising that you forgot to send that email – so you get up and send it.
- At the end of the workday you are exhausted, but you still haven't finished your tasks 'to do' for the day.
- You try to connect with work colleagues but you have a hard time finding a time that suits everyone to meet.

If you can relate to more than a couple of these points, you are working in the numb zone, and consider how many of your colleagues would be in the same position.

The numbing of people at home and at work is becoming one of the leading challenges facing the western world. We see it manifesting through the decrease in physical activity, the increase in the use of medications to help us deal with everyday life, and the realisation by many people that they are not truly fulfilled.

OVERCOMING NUMB: RECOGNISING THE PATTERN

There are ways to overcome this epidemic of numb. It's not just a question of work-life balance – that common catch cry that we need to spend more time at home than at work. I have yet to meet anyone who can successfully take more time away from work to spend at home without switching jobs or taking a decrease in pay.

What needs to happen is a change in the way we work – we need to break the autopilot cycle. It is not about decreasing our workloads or the tasks on our plates, but rather recognising our patterns of over-commitment and using strategies to overcome them. There are four common patterns: workaholic, socialite, servant and worker.

- **The Workaholic**. I remember working with a high-flying executive who was making $1 million a year. He was a classic workaholic. He and his team were putting in tremendous hours, however the stress was affecting him and his performance was starting to slide. He realised that he had been going through the motions of work just to keep busy. When I asked him why, he said that it was so he could provide a better lifestyle for his family. But unfortunately he was so self-focused that he was divorced and had a strained relationship with his kids. He wished that he could go back in time and rewrite his life. He was so numb that he hadn't seen the workaholic pattern until it was too late.
- **The Socialite**. These are the people that take on all types of community activities and then enjoy letting others know how busy and networked they are. Eventually, they also become numb – just going through the motions to make sure that others notice, but not really sharing their authentic selves with their colleagues. Often, their own families begin to resent their over-commitment.
- **The Servant**. These are the people that continually say 'yes' to additional tasks – they are the ones that other overloaded people go to to 'dump' their additional tasks on because they always say yes. After continually stressing out due to the overload, these people become numb and eventually they get so overcommitted to the community and their family that they forget who they are and what is important to them. This is a common occurrence with stay-at-home mothers who focus on their kids and the school community, and in the process realise that they don't know who they are anymore.
- **The Worker**. Not quite satisfied with things that are good, the worker is primarily focused on their family and their work. They do not really think about what they want or what direction they are taking, primarily because they are afraid of confronting themselves, which leads to them becoming numb. With their over-commitment to working the way they have always worked they also lose touch with their community, which leads to them not accepting or actively dealing with changes around them until they are forced to.

These are the common patterns that lead to the numb mind-set, where people find themselves on the mundane treadmill of existence. This occurs when we overcommit to one particular area and lose our connection with ourselves. Once you recognise these common patterns, you can begin to actively change yourself and your approach to others. Imagine working in a business full of people who were actively engaged and truly alive. It would be a wonderful place to work – and the positive effect would radiate into the community and people's home lives as well.

AVOIDING COMFORTABLY NUMB: FIVE STRATEGIES TO STAY CONNECTED

The people that have high active workloads and that are connected are truly alive! These are the people that are viewed by others as 'going somewhere', they achieve results that were not thought possible. They constantly challenge themselves and the people around them to fight the urge to go onto autopilot, and to achieve the things that are just out of reach for the numbed masses. There are five key strategies that you can use to reduce being numb and to be more connected.

1. **Being centred:** This is when you commit to being the person that you need to be. It is staying true to your path and actively choosing to live, learn, love and leave a legacy.

2. **Connect with self:** Regardless of whether you are at work or at home you have a choice to be self-focused or not. Actively remind yourself to be more aware, and stay off autopilot by recognising your pattern when you start to become numb. One of the easiest ways to avoid becoming numb is to stay physically and mentally active. When you are feeling disconnected, one of the quickest ways to recover is by taking a brisk walk or doing some exercise.

3. **Connect with family:** When we get overcommitted to ourselves, one of the important actions to take is to ground yourself with your family. Have regular check-ins with family members to give you honest feedback on where you have been focusing your time and energy. If you are truly committed to your family you will value their feedback and actively take time to be truly connected with them – without just going through the motions.

4. **Connect with colleagues:** Given that we spend most of our waking hours with our colleagues at work, it is important to truly connect with them. Actively take the time to share common experiences with them, clarify ideas and leverage opportunities.

5. **Connect with community:** Being connected to your community provides you with a deeper sense of worth. Make a choice to be involved with your community in some way. You could become more involved in your children's school, or give your time and energy to neighbours or the wider community.

Just look around and you can quickly see numb across our mental landscape. For those of you who are aspiring to be truly alive, you have an obligation to positively influence those around you to leave behind their own numbness. If we were all committed to this, we would see a radical shift in business and at home toward being a society of people that are truly connected and alive – like some people say it used to be. ●

Imagine working in a business full of people who were actively engaged and truly alive. It would be a wonderful place to work – and the positive effect would radiate into the community and people's home lives as well.

"Imagine if we knew that the people we dealt with really did care about the outcome of our situation – business would take on an entirely different paradigm."

Throughout my career people have constantly said to me, "You don't seem like a typical real estate agent". What was I supposed to be like – a horned vixen that mercilessly devoured people? Yes, I was a ruthless negotiator; yes, I was our organisation's leading female agent year after year. But what made me so un-real-estate-ish? After contemplating this question, I realised what it was that made me different: *compassion*. Yes, I cared about the deal, but more than that I cared about the people. I hold compassion as my greatest business value. What is compassion? It's empathy, sympathy, concern, kindness, consideration and care. This is considered to be completely at odds with being a successful businessperson...or is it?

doing business with heart
DEBORAH VANDERHOEK

DOING BUSINESS WITH HEART

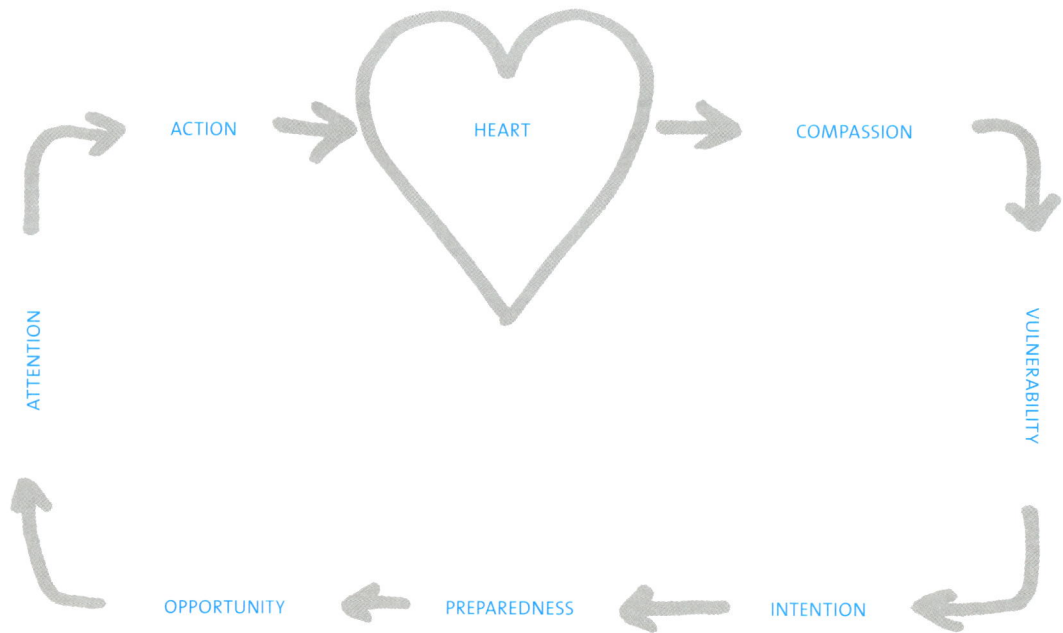

ACTION → HEART → COMPASSION

ATTENTION

VULNERABILITY

OPPORTUNITY ← PREPAREDNESS ← INTENTION

Is it possible to work from the heart – to bring a level of compassion and kindness into the workplace, to create a wonderful environment for working and living – and yet still make money?

In general, business is considered to be an unemotional transaction where the outcome is the main consideration. But what if clients were looking for something not solely based on money? What if the relationship rather than the transaction was their primary subconscious priority? What if what they really wanted was to feel nurtured, cared for and listened to? What if they were looking to be shown some kindness and consideration, and to feel 'safe' as part of the deal?

What if you were to say to your clients, "If you don't feel or think that I am doing the best for you, you can cancel our contract at any time"? Would they feel safe, would they think that you were doing business from the heart? Of course they would. And when the client feels 'safe' in the relationship, when they feel trust, the business transaction takes on a completely different paradigm.

Imagine if we all travelled through life knowing that the people we dealt with really cared about the outcome of our situation, that they cared enough to do it for free if necessary. We would have a society with a greater level of honesty, trust and cohesion. But do you think you could do that? Could you become detached from the outcome and yet still give your all to a situation? Is it possible for this to come about in a world where we are taught and trained to protect ourselves at all costs from demonstrating emotion in business, from letting people get too close to us and seeing us with all our fears and imperfections? Where would the life we know be if it were devoid of games and illusions? Is there a way to do business with heart?

DOING BUSINESS WITH HEART

There are three simple exercises that I employ to start the process of doing business with heart:

1. I always put myself in other people's shoes.
2. I approach every new relationship with positivity and honesty.
3. I have a clear intention.

I ALWAYS PUT MYSELF IN OTHER PEOPLE'S SHOES

I try to see the situation from their perspective and imagine that it is me going through the negotiation.

How do we ever know what someone else is thinking, feeling or experiencing? We don't. The best we can do is guess, judge and assume; we look for similarities with our own lives and experiences, and hope that we can come to an understanding of the other person. But the truth is that none of us is the same, and none of us reacts or responds the same way as anyone else to different circumstances – so how can we correctly assume anything? We can't.

What is compassion? It's empathy, sympathy, concern, kindness, consideration and care. This is considered to be completely at odds with being a successful businessperson...or is it?

The only way to truly come to an understanding of others is to approach each interaction from the perspective of complete openness. The person in front of us is a page written in a foreign language and the relationship becomes an adventure to discover a whole new world of another person.

As a real estate agent I often go into people's homes, and I frequently see people who seem to have no respect for the way they live – the mess, dirt and disorder is sometimes enough to make my stomach turn. From my perspective, this is not how I choose to live, but I am not them. If I were to cast my judgement I would not find the pearls lying beneath the mess. The mess is just the way they are – it is not who they are – and it has taken years and many messy houses to help me realise that it is 'just stuff' and not what is really important.

I dealt with a woman recently who had a mental illness, she was being forced to sell her home by the mortgage holder. She would hang up the phone mid-sentence as she drifted off somewhere. When I finally met her face-to-face I was consumed with compassion for her. I held her hand and told her everything would be all right. Her face became alive and alert. I sold the property for an excellent price and she is now able to get on with her life. If I had prejudged her, I would not have been given the opportunity of seeing her happy. And this, in turn, replenishes my heart.

How do you learn to bring the perspective of heart to your business dealings?

First, start listening to the language you use. Listen when you judge others. This is what I call 'pointing the finger'. Have you ever noticed when you point your finger, that there is only one finger pointing outward and three pointing back at you? Start consciously noticing when you 'point the finger' at someone else and ask yourself what signals it may be sending back to you. When I point the finger at other people's mess, it is often a signal to me that I need to let go of control, that I am being too tidy, too structured, too 'left brain' and that I need to rebalance.

Second, always clarify. Ask more questions to make sure that you have a true understanding of the other person. In sales we are trained to constantly go back and ask the client, "Are you clear?" "Is it okay?" "Did you understand what I said?" and ask them to repeat it back to you in their own words.

Third, stay flexible and open. In sales, people are so often not what they seem. I have sold a $4 million property to a young man in torn board shorts and dreadlocks, hardly a likely-looking candidate for a property of that price. When you learn to stop making judgements and start to take people for who they are a whole new dimension appears in business.

A story told to me by a very wise business mentor still resonates with me today. A man was travelling home on a train with his two children. The kids were out of control, jumping, screaming and bumping into the other passengers. A woman watched, livid, as the man peered out of the window oblivious to his children's appalling behaviour. The woman's temper started to fire and she finally tapped the man on the shoulder and said,

"Can you please keep your children under control, this is a public place". His eyes misty, and his face wrought with pain he said, "I am so sorry. We have just buried their mother". So often in life, things are not as they seem.

I APPROACH EVERY NEW RELATIONSHIP WITH POSITIVITY AND HONESTY

Positivity is a state of mind, believing that what you do, how you feel and what you think is of value. So to be positive you have to feel positive about yourself. I believe that successful business comes from within. We can all learn the scripts and dialogues but the passion, the drive, the challenge of living has to be part of ourselves. So how do we stay positive, passionate and driven? By creating balance.

I also learnt from my wise mentor that there is always someone else who can do your job – and possibly even better than you can – so give yourself freedom by empowering the people around you to discover their talents and strengths. This in turn allows you time and freedom to grow and flourish.

After years of martyrdom, believing that I was the only person who could do the deal, run the family, pick up the clothes and clean the office kitchen, and after I had become an emotional and physical wreck, I finally got it. I realised that I didn't need to be either perfect or capable of doing everything myself, and that there were so many people out there that wanted to help. So I detached. I was warned that if I was to make this huge leap my life would change and it did. My income doubled, my holiday time doubled, I started doing activities that fulfilled other aspects of my psyche. I still cared very much about the outcome of my transactions and when I worked I worked with complete focus and clarity, but I was balanced, passionate and fulfilled. I no longer hold in high regard people who say, "Oh I work so hard". Instead I feel sorry for them. I respect the people who say, "I work so smart. I spend time with my children, I take family holidays, I help my spouse, I have fun and am passionate about my profession". Workaholics are out, this is the age of smartaholics.

An intrinsic part of creating balance and working with purpose is honesty. I was told by a lawyer friend when I decided to get into real estate that it was a bad Karmic profession. That it was based on lies and deception. Being honest can sometimes cause pain, granted, but being dishonest to either your clients or yourself is tragic.

Too many people hold back information, both good and bad, from their clients. If you are detached from the outcome and if you truly care about what they are going through, being completely honest without fear of reprisals is essential. I have occasionally had to share bad news with clients in circumstances such as where there is no buyer for their home, even after they've spent many thousands of dollars on advertising, had people traipsing through their home at open houses for months and feel emotionally stripped bare. And while they will understandably feel anger about the outcome, it's not directed at me because by that stage in the transaction the relationship is so strong that they know I have done everything I can. I have never had a client walk away feeling or thinking that I have let them down.

Ironically, the money always takes care of itself if your focus is on the people not the outcome. The tighter you hold onto a situation, the worse the outcome. When you are detached and operating with care, compassion and honesty the outcome is generally favourable.

This method of doing business might seem simple, but unfortunately business is NOT generally conducted from the heart with honesty, and 'vulnerability' is often considered a dirty word.

I HAVE A CLEAR INTENTION

Do you know what you want? When I started in business I knew that I wanted to be the best. I wanted to win awards. I had no experience but I had a clear intention and purpose, I had a goal. No different from Cathy Freeman running the 400 metres in 49.11 seconds. Four years before, at the Atlanta Olympics, she wrote down that time and manifested her intention – to the exact millisecond.

The mind is very helpful *if* you have a clear intention. But people so often drift from situation to situation, letting obstacles get in their way. A clear purpose is like a train track, if there is no track, the train is forced to stop

In my first few years of business my goals and intentions were clear. I wrote a list of everything I wanted to achieve, a 'wish list'. This supposedly unattainable list was lost in a house move and I didn't find it again until four years later. What amazed me was that of the 20 or so items that I had dreamt of achieving, I had achieved 18 of them, and those that I hadn't achieved, I really didn't want to. This simple exercise confirmed to me just how powerful our mind is if we have a clear intent and are prepared to act on it.

My purpose now is to bring heart into business. To show by example that it is possible to be compassionate, kind, considerate, truthful, vulnerable and successful, focused and driven. To prove that they are not contradictions, but fundamentals to doing business in the 21st century.

THE HEART

Overriding all of this is the most important factor – the heart. Without our hearts we are cold, uncaring, selfish creatures that merely survive. Compassion and heart fills us with extraordinary power, a universal power to achieve extraordinary things. It creates a very strange yet powerful reciprocity. People start to talk about you, they want you around, you make them feel good about themselves, and they feel safe and loved.

After years of enjoying boundless success, earning more money than I ever expected I could earn, staying in five-star hotels that I never imagined I could stay in and enjoying a life so truly filled with abundance and love, my beliefs were tested. Having breakfast on a tropical island during a family vacation my untainted world collapsed. The tsunami hit the little seaside village of Unawatuna in Sri Lanka. Within seconds my husband, children, mother and friends were running for their lives. Screams of despair, death and destruction filled the air as the water took everything in its path. We miraculously survived; 30,000 people around us did not. When faced with life or death it is life, and the people in it who count.

So, whether I sell a home worth $500,000 or $5 million I realise that the bricks and mortar are replaceable – the people, their dreams and their memories are not. It is the people that matter. I continue to allow the seeds of compassion, kindness and vulnerability to grow in every transaction and relationship that I engage in and remain committed to doing business with heart. ☙

"**Most of us have enough great ideas to keep us busy for a lifetime – yet too few of us are brave enough to persist and make them happen.**"

The greater our idea potential (which I like to call 'IP') the bigger the anti-creators we face. Anti-creators are disproportionately greater than our IP. For example, an everyday idea such as trying a new meal for dinner, or finding a new angle on a project, has generally low anti-creator resistance. An inspirational idea that may involve a fair amount of time and resources will have intimidating anti-creators. And when we come up with a revolutionary, life-changing idea we can find that the anti-creators become overwhelming. Understanding each of the anti-creators not only reduces their size, but also makes getting past them that much easier and more enjoyable.

stop talking, start creating
NILS VESK

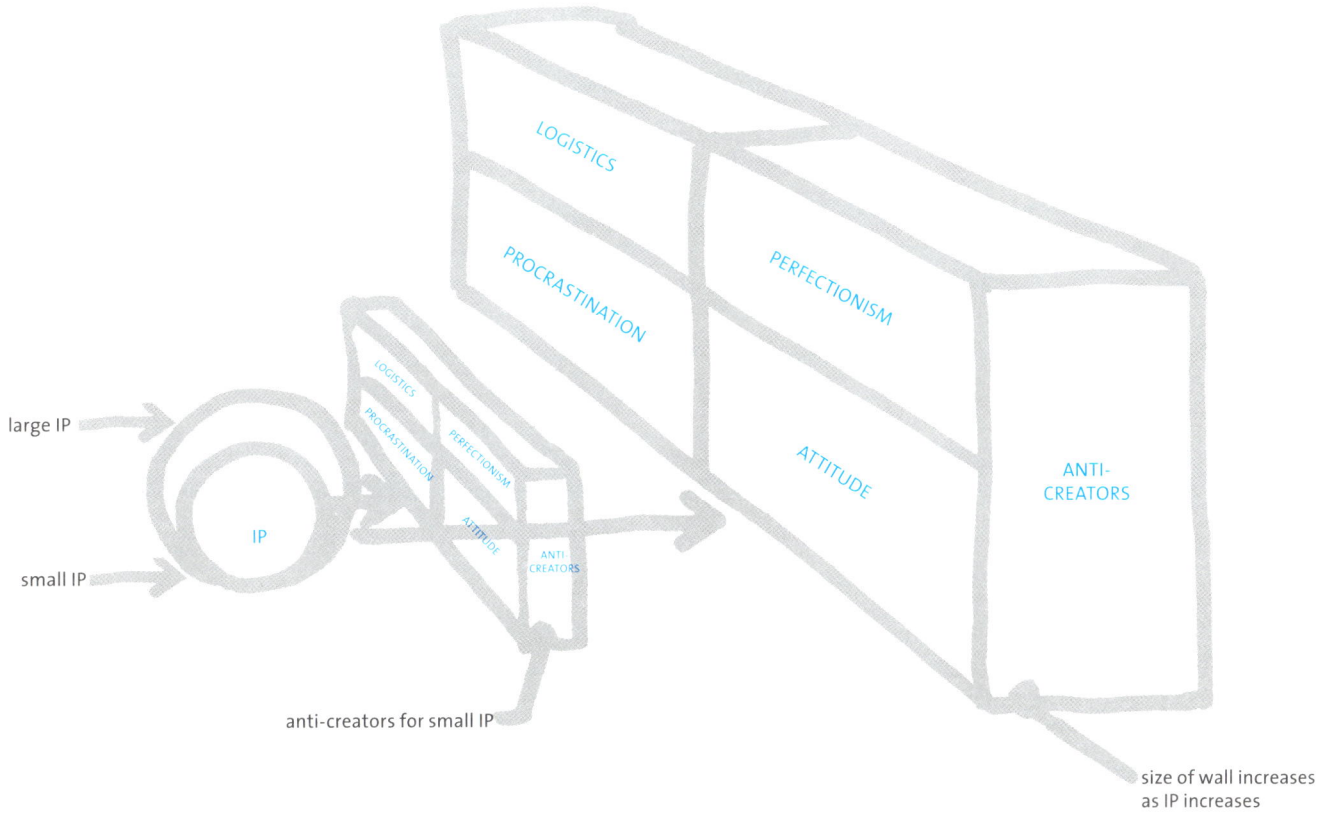

large IP

small IP

IP

anti-creators for small IP

LOGISTICS

PROCRASTINATION

PERFECTIONISM

ATTITUDE

ANTI-CREATORS

size of wall increases
as IP increases

THE WALLS WE ALL ENCOUNTER

There are four main anti-creators that we all face when trying to turn our ideas into reality:

1. Logistics
2. Perfectionism
3. Procrastination
4. Attitude

These are not exclusive to the 'creation' process, so learning how to deal with them will not only help us in realising our ideas, but will also help in many other areas of our lives. So let's get on with it.

ANTI-CREATOR NO. 1: LOGISTICS

Most of us are familiar with the term 'logistics' and understand logistical issues, such as how to get something from A to B. Many of us will also experience (at some point) a logistical barrier to getting our ideas completed – no time, no money and no idea are logistical excuses that we hear often. All idea realisations require logistics at some time, so let's nail this one first.

Take less, give more: We can't create more time, but we can use our time more effectively. The less time you give yourself to complete a task the more chance you have of completing it. Invariably, we all run over deadlines, so by setting tighter timeframes we can achieve more in less time.

Speak French: Designers use the term 'Charette' to describe the quick drawings used to communicate ideas. Legend has it that the word's origin comes from an old Parisian university where an elderly assistant would wheel a cart around collecting drawings that needed to be submitted at the end of each year. The old man would call out "Char-ette, Char-ette" – literally meaning 'put with the cart'. You can bet that after two years of working on their projects the students put enormous effort into those last few minutes to get the job done.

Create a 'charette' around your idea right now. Give yourself two minutes to work on your idea as though it were the last opportunity you'll get. The more 'charettes' you give yourself, the more you'll get done.

> Giving yourself an 'lifeline' is a positive spin on the dreaded term, 'deadline'. When you've set your 'lifeline' date, remember that it's the opportunity to bring your ideas to fruition and the beginning of something, not the end.

Get a date then a life: Having a date is one of the key elements to bringing an idea to life. Our date helps provide part of our idea contract and ensures that we are kept accountable and motivated to make it happen. Giving yourself an 'lifeline' is a positive spin on the dreaded term, 'deadline'. When you've set your 'lifeline' date, remember that it's the opportunity to bring your ideas to fruition and the beginning of something, not the end.

Know-how is show-how: The magic behind realising ideas is in being able to visualise them and the tasks that need to be completed to make them happen. The more we are able to 'see' what it is that needs to be done, the easier it is to organise and execute the idea. And the more people involved in bringing the idea to fruition, the better we need to be at communicating, showing and organising so that the right people are doing the right things with the right tools.

Knowledge: We think it's too hard, we don't know the answers, and we feel like giving up. It's not going to get any easier unless we claim our ignorance and ask for enlightenment. As soon as we identify our problems and ask questions things start getting easier.

Dumb up: The more we claim what we don't know, the clearer the path becomes. The more questions we ask of ourselves and others, the sooner we find the answers. The next time you're stuck, write down the problem or the questions you need answered; often the question is the answer in disguise.

Wise up: Looking for answers means research, and the better the questions we have the easier it is to get the research right. Many of the answers we need are available to us at the click of a finger. Search engines are fast and effective knowledge hunters at our disposal. Some services include: www.google.com/answers, www.answers.com, www.elibrary.com, and www.inquisit.com.

An overarching solution can be found in outsourcing. Outsource whatever you're stuck on and you'll find life becomes easier even though it comes at a price. The cheapest, most accessible outsourcing directory around the globe is www.elance.com. Try it.

Make it up: There are times when we just have to make it up ourselves because no one has taken the path before. Our intuition can often be our best ally when stuck for what to do. Ask your intuition what to do next and try it. Ponder for a moment on how much of what you have created in the past involved just making it up as you go along – so, why not try it again now?

Steal more money: Rearranging our finances is something that often needs to be done to fund our ideas. We may need to pinch a bit from our entertainment account, start taking more lunches to work, or even put the house up for refinancing. Finding money is mostly a matter of rearranging priorities. Think about where you could get the money if you really needed it.

Borrow deep: There are ways of funding your ideas by getting money from third parties – all it takes is you, the idea, the ability to communicate your vision and the right venture capitalist or business partner. When we play their game we need to be able to communicate in their language. Communicating your idea by starting with, "It's sort of like…" will help them to make sense of what you want to create. It's vital that you're able to communicate your idea in such a way that they 'get it'. From an investor's perspective, if you can't describe it clearly, that's probably a good reason for it not having been created before.

Be poor: We've all seen how ingenious people become when they have very few options. What can you do with what you've got? Can you get your idea to a prototype stage? Can you substitute the materials or elements for something less expensive? The more we see it is a matter of subsistence in trying to get food on the table and a roof over our heads, the more creative we become in dealing with money challenges.

ANTI-CREATOR NO. 2: PERFECTIONISM

Perfection is a major paradigm that affects creating in a big way. There are benefits of striving for perfectionism in quality, yet the control mind-set that can come with perfectionism can also cause paralysis, fear, anxiety and an unwillingness to try new things. The right time and place for perfectionism is in the tail end of the creation process, not in the beginning when it can prevent something from happening. When we feel perfectionism getting in the way we need to throw it out. How?

Death is guaranteed but realising ideas isn't: Perfectionism is a block to many would-be creators. Perfectionists have it all worked out, except for knowing what the outcome will be. The truth is that even the best creations change all the time, and the market may love or hate your idea – either way you win because you can move on to improve it or disregard it.

Reality sucks: Living in a perfect world 24/7 is impossible. We, and everyone around us, make mistakes of some kind every day. Sure, we can achieve moments of perfection, but the perfectionist striving for nirvana will be constantly shot to pieces by their own excessive judgement and the fear of beginning ideas that have every right to succeed. Look for evidence that perfectionism is impossible and that even the most successful people make mistakes. Even major manufacturers have a failure rate factored into their manufacturing process. They expect roughly in the order of three to five per cent of things to fail. If it's good enough for them, it's good enough for us. Create your own failure rate, and if you're not meeting it then you're probably not producing enough!

Be rough: Adopting a 'draft' mind-set can really help perfectionists to move through the wall. The next report you do or the next idea you have, stamp it 'DRAFT' and notice how much more you can get done without the anxiety of perfectionism. The draft mentality is what helps convert perfect into prolific. Picasso produced on average one painting a day for his entire adult life, definitely prolific not perfect.

ANTI-CREATOR NO. 3: PROCRASTINATION

Procrastination is self-induced, self-administered and self-defeating. It's a part of us that is stopping us from moving forward. Every time a procrastination pops up, see it as a gremlin, give it the finger, say something aloud like, "You won't stop me from making it happen!", and take immediate action to do something toward your idea realisation.

Watch the clock: Procrastination takes a whole lot of time, so much so that we don't know where it goes. How much time do you spend avoiding getting on with the job? Write out what you spend your time procrastinating on, what it prevents you from starting and what the consequences of your procrastination will be – that should give you the motivation you need to get moving.

No matter what: Create a 'we'll do it now' mind-set, because tomorrow may never come. If you step it up even further into an 'I'm going to do this even if it kills me' mind-set, that really helps us to challenge our procrastination.

Get high: One of the drivers behind our procrastination is the discomfort we experience in doing something new, different, challenging or difficult. The rub is that creating ideas isn't always easy, if it was everyone would be doing it. Most of us have a low frustration tolerance in at least a couple of areas in our lives. Yet, procrastination is built around the amount of frustration that comes with it. The higher the frustration, the more we procrastinate, and the lower our tolerance to frustration, the less likely we are to make our idea happen. The best way to get a high tolerance to frustration is by immersing yourself in it. Try this now. Imagine a task that you often procrastinate, such as going to the dentist, doing your tax return and so on. Close your eyes and scan your body. Imagine doing the task, turn up the intensity, and stick with the discomfort. Now imagine it done, how does it feel? Now imagine starting it again and see if the intensity has changed – then, get to it on the real thing.

ANTI-CREATOR NO. 4: ATTITUDE

Our attitude is a combination of our internal and external worlds. Our internal world is made up of our self-talk, beliefs and self-image, while our external world is made up of our physiology (body language), communication (words), the things we do (actions), our commitment and our results. Is your attitude preventing you from realising your ideas?

Split from the past: Changing what we do now compared to what we've done in the past is vital if we want to move forward with our ideas. Changing how we think and do things is a great step to getting the right attitude for creating. Replacing negative words such as 'can't', 'should', 'must' and 'have to' with positives such as 'can', 'could', 'want to', 'like to' and 'I am doing this'

helps to flip the mind-set. If you have made up stories in the past that aren't working for you, create new ones that do. Create a new story today about you as a successful creator and start living that life fully.

Stop getting run over: Our thoughts drive our feelings and emotions, and the more wayward the thoughts the more wayward the results. If we can get ourselves thinking right rather than wrong we can fix the feelings and the behaviours. The psychologist Albert Ellis developed a cognitive behaviour model that many modern psychologists use today. Next time you find yourself saying, "It's too hard", use the ABCs and write down:

Adversity – the events that are happening, for example 'I'm not working on my idea'.

Beliefs – the things you make up about yourself, such as 'I'm not smart enough', 'It's too hard', and 'It sucks'.

Consequences – what will happen if you keep thinking this way, for example will you give up or feel miserable?

Dispute – what evidence can you find to disprove these beliefs, such as listing your previous successes, qualifications or experience; or the times that you've applied yourself with a mind-set to get something done? Then create a real disputing statement based on these facts, for example, 'I have the ability, determination and resources at my disposal to make this happen'.

Energy – How do you feel now? Better? If so, get into it!

Failure is fun: We all stuff-up, but the stuff-ups are more fun if we celebrate them and see what we have learnt from them. The more we embrace them as a part of the idea process, the more we reduce the fear of failure

Take a walk: Obstacles are best faced with a fresh perspective. Taking a look at the obstacle from a new perspective enables us to see things with fresh eyes and spot new opportunities or directions that we can take to move our idea along.

Get on with it: Now that we've taken a few steps together to challenge our anti-creators it's time to get onto our ideas.

Remember, it's only the anti-creators stopping us, no major war just an internal battle that can be won, so charge! ❷

"Trainers train programs, about which they know lots, for customers about whom they know little, and in organisations about which they know even less."

(apologies to Voltaire)

The current business model for Learning and Development (L&D) is not suited to success in the future – we haven't been successful in the past, with up to 80 per cent of the learning investment in training being wasted. Changes are needed that involve L&D becoming inextricably linked to senior managements' perception and achievement of the organisation's bottom line. L&D is no longer just in the realm of HR; it is a business imperative for which all trainers, executives, business owners and managers need to take responsibility.

no more mr nice guy
MARK WAYLAND

AN UNBALANCED BUSINESS MODEL FOR LEARNING AND DEVELOPMENT

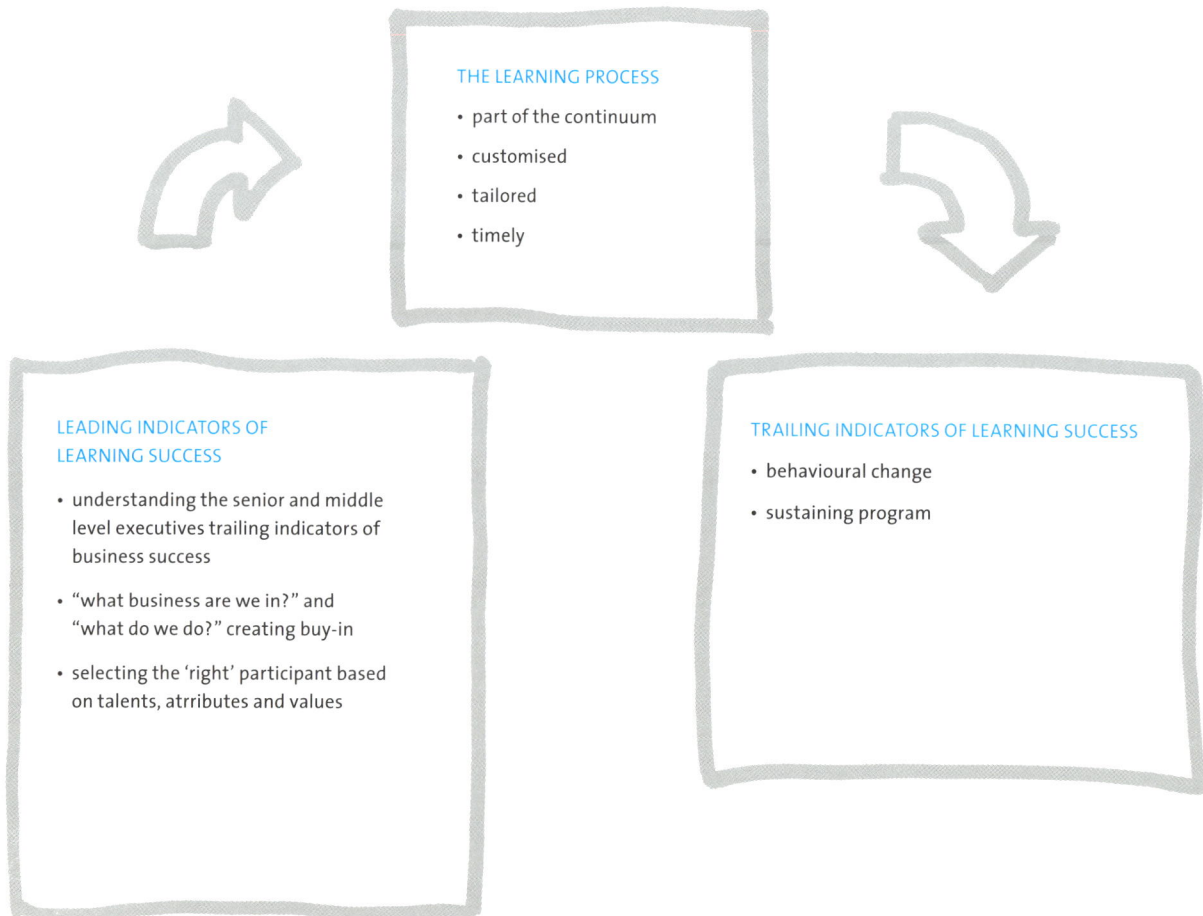

THE LEARNING PROCESS

- part of the continuum
- customised
- tailored
- timely

LEADING INDICATORS OF LEARNING SUCCESS

- understanding the senior and middle level executives trailing indicators of business success
- "what business are we in?" and "what do we do?" creating buy-in
- selecting the 'right' participant based on talents, atrributes and values

TRAILING INDICATORS OF LEARNING SUCCESS

- behavioural change
- sustaining program

I'm a learning and development 'tragic'. I'm obsessed with improving the way mainstream businesspeople and trainers perceive learning and development (L&D) and how they can use it more effectively and for much better outcomes. This obsession started building a few years ago over two different lunches with two different people. Both were to have a dramatic effect on my perception of my profession.

At the first lunch, a very senior manager shared his big picture view of our organisation with me. "It was," he said, "tribal by nature, with three distinct groups of people in three distinct roles". He went onto explain them:

• The **Elders** are the people with many years of experience and expertise, wisdom and cunning. They are the senior managers who provide the strategic direction and guidance for the business.
• The **Hunters** are the people who bring in the revenue of the organisation. They are the sales and marketing teams that drive the business.
• The **Camp Followers** make up the remainder of the organisation's personnel. They are the shared services that support the business and are the organisation's cost centres.

It was this senior manager's opinion that L&D was a 'Camp Follower'. Considering how hard the L&D team worked and the reputation we had earned for the world-class standard of training we delivered, I was shocked. No, more than that, it made me feel that we were undervalued and deserved more respect for our contribution to the organisation's vision and mission. But as he continued to speak I began to understand that his perception of us, and what we did, was the company's reality.

"Well," he said, "there's nobody from training at the board or senior management meetings, so it's not an 'Elder'. It doesn't help drive the business, so it's not a 'Hunter'. It supports the business, so it's a 'Camp Follower'".

He saw the look on my face and said, "Don't get me wrong. The L&D team's work is highly valued and recognised as an important business element. But in all reality, I can't see how it would be put on the same strategic level as sales and marketing".

The second lunch was with Brett Godfrey, CEO of the airline, Virgin Blue. The ultimate measure of their business success, he said, was the number of people flying with Virgin Blue. There were three kinds of measures he could get:
• how many people flew Virgin Blue yesterday, last week or last month
• how many are flying today, and
• how many will be flying tomorrow, next week or next month.

He explained that the first kind of data simply gave him bragging rights. It's history. Managing the company using historical figures (no matter how recent) is reactive and fraught with difficulties. As far as knowing what's happening today, that's interesting but you can't do much about increasing today's figures today. What you can do much more about is trying to create the kind of tomorrow, next week and next month you want by managing those activities and behaviours today that will surely lead to success.

It made me realise that managing the leading indicators of business performance is far more powerful than trying to manage from the trailing indicators. After 25 years' involvement with all aspects of L&D, from the delivery of programs through to managing a team of trainers in both government and corporate arenas, I realised that we, as a professional group, are fixated by the learning event and that we're bogged down by the 'support service' mentality.

Then I came across a book that made me realise that the current business model for L&D really needed to be revamped. It was Broad and Newstrom's *Transfer of Training*. In it they say, 'Most of the investment in organisational training and development is wasted because most of the knowledge and skills gained in training (well over 80 per cent by some estimates) is not fully applied by those employees on the job'. Now, I knew that L&D wasn't perfect, but 80 per cent wastage?!

This wastage occurs because of a combination of different factors, some of which L&D people can control, some they can't, and some they need to learn how to control. With some effort I believe that L&D can not only be far more efficient and effective, but that it can also lift its standing within the business community as a driver of business success.

Let's first of all be perfectly clear about one thing. L&D should really have only one meaningful goal: getting participants to change their behaviour once they return to work.

And there are only three things that affect the achievement of this goal:
1. The design and delivery of the training program.
2. The climate in the workplace that provides a context for change and encourages the opportunity to change.
3. The participants' talents, values and attributes.

THE DESIGN AND DELIVERY OF THE TRAINING PROGRAM

This is the technical expertise that L&D professionals have and are recognised for. Trainers though, are too concerned with the 'learning event' and the need to engage the learner. They then try to provide various quantitative measures that provide evidence of L&D's value and contribution to business units. Our methodology has been to try and educate our many masters and partners in 'what we do' – our operational efficiency – using L&D theory and jargon that is off-putting. We reason that once 'they' understand the world from our perspective, they'll see just how valuable a contribution we make.

We think that the learner is our main customer, that it's the learner and the learning process that we need to know most about. It was the American, Zig Ziglar, who famously said, "If you keep doing what you've been doing, you keep getting what you've been getting". It's time to stop getting only the 20 per cent return we've been getting by shifting what we've been doing and altering the context for the design and delivery of the training program by including a forgotten customer.

The opportunity for L&D is to include the various senior and middle level executives as our customers. We should be showing them that we understand how L&D can best be aligned with the various strategies of the business and its changing needs. L&D professionals need to show that they are also capable of looking at the organisation from 10,000 feet (that is, taking the big picture view), anticipating and putting strategies in place to meet the changing needs of the organisation and its people: we need to help drive the business of an organisation.

The focus of L&D must be broadened. By all means, keep taking quantitative measures to show value and how training programs complement business unit goals, but L&D should also focus more on the leading indicators of business success, proactively identify issues that are speed bumps to organisational success and help to drive solutions.

> Trainers need to find out what business numbers, indicators, processes and outcomes managers use to measure productivity, customer satisfaction and profitability, and then determine the equivalent in L&D behaviours that drive performance.

Rather than educating 'Elders' and 'Hunter' managers about the L&D perspective, trainers should be talking to them about results and outcomes, not just outputs. Many managers get stuck in the rut of only reviewing the numbers (trailing indicators) without analysing the underlying issues that drive performance (leading indicators). These managers are looking for ways to increase revenue without increasing expenses, and for ways to reduce the time it takes for employees to master new skills/processes and create a competitive edge. They are also very concerned with maintaining shareholder value. Trainers need to find out what business numbers, indicators, processes and outcomes managers use to measure productivity, customer satisfaction and profitability, and then determine the equivalent in L&D behaviours that drive performance. Then we can demonstrate how L&D has qualitatively aligned its initiatives with the changing needs of the business. In short, we need to show what L&D is capable of doing that makes a difference to the organisation's bottom line.

Expanding L&D's perspective from quantitative value measurements of trailing indicators of success, toward embracing qualitative alignment and integration of L&D initiatives with leading indicators of business success is a sure way of strengthening L&D's strategic position within the organisation.

THE CLIMATE IN THE WORKPLACE THAT PROVIDES A CONTEXT FOR CHANGE

Broad and Newstrom point out that what happens before and after training is at least as important as what happens during the learning event. I agree with them that trainers need to expand their roles and be much more active in the 'before' and 'after' in some form of partnership with the participants' manager. It seems that the role of the manager/trainer partnership is to get better buy-in from the participant in the learning process and to sustain the changes in behaviour back in the workplace.

I've found that a major issue in accomplishing this is that many managers (at all levels) have lost the ability to clearly communicate and distinguish between the two major aspects of their business: 'what business are we in?' and 'what do we do?' As I mentioned, many managers get stuck in the rut of only reviewing the numbers that measure the 'what do we do', without analysing the underlying issues of 'what business are we in' that drive performance.

What business are we in? These are the more emotional, attitudinal, perceptual, inspirational and values-driven aspects of an organisation. It reflects the 'soft' aspects of business branding and is the foundation for the uniqueness of the organisation, customer and employee loyalty. It's doing the 'right' things.

What do we do? Reflects the factual, logical, operational and transactional aspects of an organisation. It reflects the 'hard' aspects of numbers, profitability, cash flow and margins. It's doing things 'right'.

Put another way, if there's to be a change in behaviour, participants not only need to know what they are expected to do differently but also the context of why this is important. They need the opportunity to reconcile their part in contributing to 'what business are we in'. Understanding the context of the training creates personal ownership of the change. Not addressing the emotional aspects of training creates resistance; participants feel that they are being pressured into (and may be the victims of) an unnecessary change. Then they need to be supported by trainers and managers as they consolidate the change. Employees that have both a high buy-in and agreement with 'what business are we in' and knowledge of 'what do we do' become amazingly high producers for the business.

L&D is no longer just in the realm of HR. It is an important business imperative that all executives, business owners and managers have responsibility for.

THE PARTICIPANTS' TALENTS, ATTRIBUTES AND VALUES

My own anecdotal evidence points to many reasons why participants are selected for training programs. They range from being a reward, an inducement to join the organisation, or a staff retention tool, to the traditional professional development for skill enhancement and promotion purposes. I've also seen training programs used as conference time-fillers and justifiers of a day spent on the golf course, as well as bona fide learning experiences.

Not so long ago training was all about developing skill sets. In fact, traditionally in recruitment potential employees have been desirable because of the skills they brought with them, only to be sacked months later because they didn't have the right attitudes, attributes or values that the organisation wanted. Skill sets and talents are related to 'what do we do' while attitudes and values are related to 'what business are we in'.

Managers find it relatively easy to list, monitor and measure the behaviours that are associated with the skills and talents of 'what do we do'. And trainers find it easy to train these behaviours. The challenge for both managers and trainers is in determining the behaviours that clearly and authentically show the values, attributes and attitudes needed to support 'what business are we in'. They are associated with the behaviours for the leading indicators of business success and relate to values and attributes such as adaptability, resilience (as in Emotional Intelligence), resourcefulness and awareness of opportunities. The challenge is met when managers, trainers and participants all contribute to behavioural descriptors of 'what a good job looks like'. These job descriptors then become a coaching and recruitment tool, and even a tool for determining incentives.

I know that by understanding the executive, business owner and management perspectives, by working toward integrating learning outcomes with the drivers of business outcomes, and by being proactive and agile in identifying future business needs, L&D will become far more aligned with the mainstream elements within the organisation.

I can see it now: the CEO is planning a meeting about a new direction or initiative for the business. He says to his PA, "Get the board members together and make sure the heads of sales, marketing, and learning and development are there as well". 🖉

> I know that by understanding the executive, business owner and management perspectives, by working toward integrating learning outcomes with the drivers of business outcomes, and by being proactive and agile in identifying future business needs, L&D will become far more aligned with the mainstream elements within the organisation.

"Four billion dollars is spent by Australian businesses each year on training – of that, two billion dollars is completely wasted."

According to research, as little as 10 to 20 per cent of all training is ever transferred from the training room into the workplace. It's not that participants don't leave training courses inspired, motivated and committed to implementing new ways of doing things, but rather that when they return to the workplace, faced with the usual challenges and constraints of the day, that motivation fades and they quickly fall back into old habits and established ways of behaving. As business is beginning to understand, training programs are just the beginning of the learning process – to fully realise the benefits of staff training we need to begin thinking of the training program itself as just the first step.

turning learning into action™
EMMA WEBER

THE COMPONENTS OF LEARNING

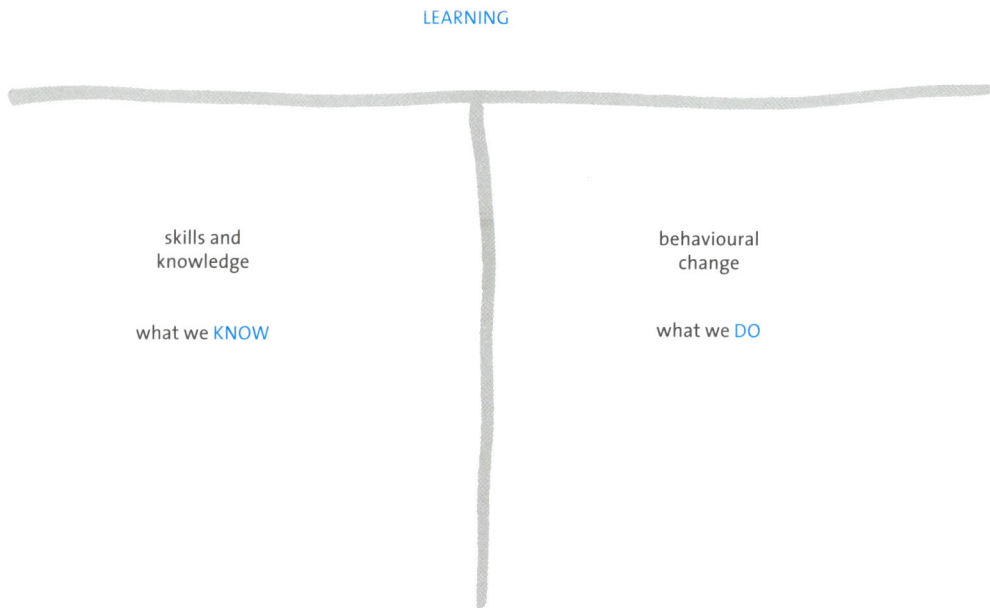

LEARNING

skills and
knowledge

what we KNOW

behavioural
change

what we DO

THE MISSING LEARNING LINK

Training design has improved markedly over the last decade, and most professional training programs today make very effective use of adult learning principles. In fact, teaching techniques are often so effective in building skills and knowledge that participants retain the content long after the training program has finished. However, there is a key component missing in most training programs.

There are two distinct components to learning:
• skills and knowledge
• behavioural change

Or put another way:
• what we know
• what we actually do

While training is a very effective way to teach skills and knowledge it is inherently limited in its effectiveness in securing long-term behavioural change. Most companies invest heavily in the skills and knowledge component, but fail to invest in the behavioural change component. All that is needed to rectify the problem, and to help companies reap the rewards of their training investment, is the understanding that while skills and knowledge can be learnt in the training room an investment in the post-training period, where behavioural change is secured, is also required.

MAKING A CHANGE IS EASY…IT'S JUST A WHOLE LOT EASIER NOT TO

Change can happen in an instant. Occasionally, a person will read something in a book or meet an individual who has such a huge impact on them that they change instantly and effortlessly. More often however, change takes place over a longer period of time.

After attending a training course and learning new skills and knowledge, people return to the workplace and try to use that learning to change a habit – whether we're trying to give up smoking or to change any of our workplace behaviours the challenge is the same, and it is rarely successful. While the catalyst for change may certainly occur during a training course, a continued effort is required over a period of weeks to ensure that the change is permanent.

THE STAGES OF LEARNING

You may be familiar with the learning model in which training takes an individual from being in a state of unconscious incompetence (that is, they don't realise what they don't know until it is pointed out to them), to a state of conscious incompetence. This is the stage at which participants faced with new realisations often comment, "Wow, I never knew it could be done like that". The next stage is conscious competence, where participants know what to do, and if they remain focused are able to do it. The key to successful training however, is when participants get to the final stage, where they are unconsciously competent – that is, they can use the new skill and knowledge without even thinking about it – it has become a habit. To create habits takes a longer period of time than it does to learn new skills and knowledge, and so there is clearly a gap between the end of the learning cycle and the development of a new behavioural habit.

BARRIERS TO CHANGE

Let's briefly look at four of the primary barriers to change that people face back in the workplace after a training program:
• **Urgency:** Typically, after having been away from the office for a training program, a backlog of work awaits us upon our return. 'Catching up' becomes the top priority and once back in the flow of everyday office activity the training course quickly becomes a memory.

- **Comfort zone:** The familiar office environment represents a comfort zone, and although it's easy to experiment and try new things while away from this environment the impetus to change often wanes when back in familiar surroundings.
- **Reflection:** Reflection is a key component of adult learning, looking at what has gone well and what could be done differently next time is a very valuable process, yet this is rarely achieved without some external stimuli.
- **Support:** Managers and colleagues do not support change. Even the best managers will often only have a hurried conversation with an individual asking them for feedback on the training course, which does nothing to secure change. Also, back in the workplace participants are surrounded by colleagues who are used to them behaving in the 'old' way and they don't generally support an individual's attempts to try out their new behaviours.

SO WHAT CAN BE DONE TO OVERCOME THESE BARRIERS?

There are two main strategies that can be implemented to overcome the challenge of wasted training dollars. They are the development and use of:

1. Action Plans
2. Action Sessions

ACTION PLANS

Action Plans are often completed by participants at the end of the training course and are intended to detail the key goals or targets that he or she wants to implement back in the workplace as a result of what has been learnt. But unfortunately, back in the workplace these Action Plans rarely leave the training folder and are never implemented.

Part of the problem is the way that 'next steps' sessions are incorporated into training programs. It is usually something done as a group activity with the trainer, and is generally done as an afterthought or formality rather than as a key component of the training itself. It's also usually done at the end of the course when participants are low in energy and counting down the minutes until they can head home. For trainers, the process finishes once the training program is complete but for participants it is just the beginning, so in order to establish the foundations for lasting behavioural change to occur post-training, a new approach from trainers to gaining 'next step' commitments is essential.

At their most effective, Action Plans can be specifically designed to increase the level of implementation by ensuring that they are driven by the individual and that they are targeting work that can be owned by him or her. While the chosen actions need to be in line with the company's goals, first and foremost they need to be actions that the individual believes will assist them in their role.

It is often said that it is not the goal that motivates an individual but the 'why' that sits behind it. So, individuals need to get really clear on 'why' the action is so important for them – this creates leverage for change.

It is also important to consider how many behaviours can be effectively changed following a single training course. I often hear participants and trainers say, "If you take just one thing away from this training course then that's great," but in my opinion, if a participant has invested two days in a training course they really want to be taking more than one new skill away with them. Ideally, individuals should be aiming to nominate three actions for implementation back in the workplace following a training course.

> Action Sessions ensure that the Action Plan implementation process gains momentum over time.

Once the Action Plan is in place, it is the Action Process that works to secure lasting behavioural change. One of the simplest ways to improve the use of Action Plans is for individuals to place their plans in their diary or on their desk where they are visible and easily revisited every day. The plan therefore needs to be in a format that encourages this, such as on a page that can be removed from the training workbook or manual, rather than something created and stored electronically.

ACTION SESSIONS

Action Sessions ensure that the Action Plan implementation process gains momentum over time. Ideally, an individual would be supported for six to eight weeks following a training program, by which time they will have been able to change old habits and replace them with the new learnings. Action Sessions may be delivered face-to-face, by telephone or by email – the important thing is that they are regular and repeated.

The ACTION process

Before we look at how Action Sessions work, let's look at the stages of the ACTION process:

A –   An **accountability** structure is created for the implementation process.

C –   Goals are set and **calibrated** post-training by the participant, defining how they will use their new skills.

T –   The **target** is identified in each Action Session – participants know what they are aiming for.

I –   They reflect and gather **information** about what is happening in the workplace to assess accurately where they are now.

O –   The **options** are brainstormed to plan a way forward.

N –   Commitment for the **next steps** that will take place in between Action Sessions is gained and monitored. This secures a behavioural change owned completely by the participant.

Why does the ACTION process work so well?

The key points that Action Sessions address, and the reason for their effectiveness, is that they:

- give the participant a structured opportunity to reflect on and review their progress
- act as a sounding board to help the participant identify solutions that overcome the challenges they face in implementing their new skills and knowledge
- keep the new skill or knowledge in the forefront of the participant's mind
- encourage the participant to look closely at what is holding them back
- assist the participant in measuring and monitoring their success

- act as a supportive cheerleader to help participants stay motivated toward making positive changes
- effectively deliver change implementation in a way that suits the individual and his or her role and circumstances.

HOW TO MAKE IT HAPPEN

The flexibility of Action Session delivery means that companies have great flexibility in how they are conducted and by whom. Many companies assume that the responsibility lies with participants' managers, which is often a mistake as managers are generally not appropriately skilled, or lack the time, to provide this vital support. In addition, due to the nature of the relationship between a manager and staff member, the manager is generally placed in the role of being the 'expert', which immediately reduces the ownership and level of change that the individual takes responsibility for. Not only this, but staff members are often reluctant to openly admit their weaknesses to their managers for fear of impacting their future prospects within the organisation. A more effective way to engage managers in helping staff to implement new behaviours is to match participants with managers from other parts of the organisation who do not have a bearing on their day-to-day role and future career prospects.

When companies are clear on the differences between the skills and knowledge component of training and the behavioural change component, they can identify ways to better manage it, whether it is through up-skilling managers, incorporating it as part of the HR function or outsourcing the role to a specialist company.

THE BOTTOM LINE

By considering the two distinct components involved in learning – skills and knowledge, and behavioural change – there is much that companies can do to reverse the trend of wasted training dollars and begin creating real results from their training investment by turning all company learning into action.

"Innovation begins with an attitude and a willingness to embrace the unknown. And when you focus on making your ideas happen, you start to become an intrapreneur."

Closely resembling entrepreneurs, we call the people who turn ideas into realities within an organisation 'intrapreneurs' – they are the hands-on 'doers' who make new ideas happen. They roll up their sleeves to get things done and recruit others to assist them. They are the dreamers who do – either building on someone else's ideas or creating their own.

the dreamers who do
BELINDA YABSLEY

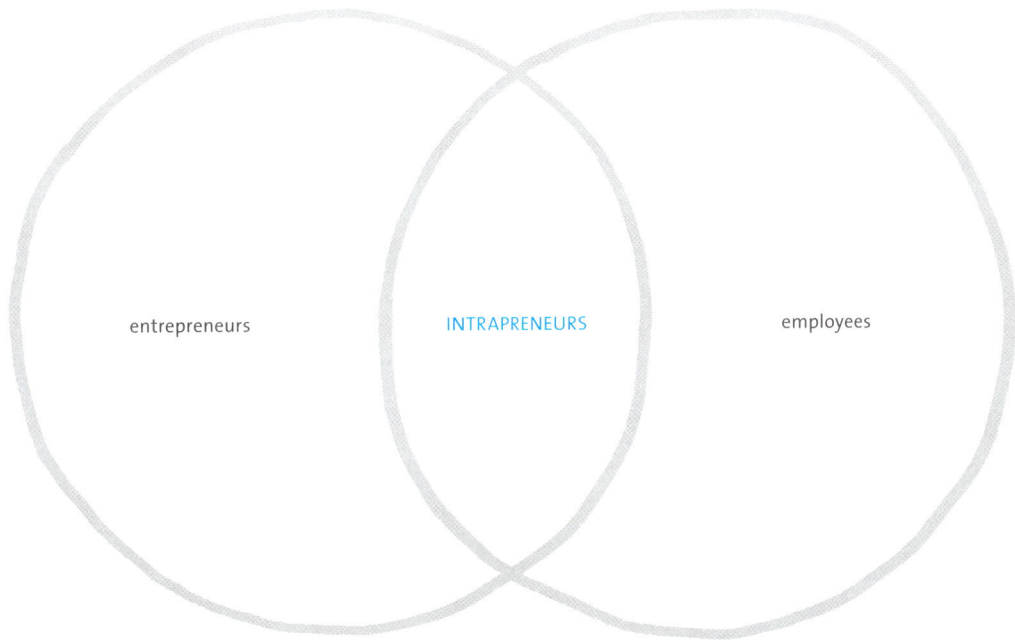

entrepreneurs

INTRAPRENEURS

employees

I began my career in the automotive industry in 1992. When I left business college I took up a position as receptionist with York Motors where I began my first database. I used index cards to record special notes that would make it easier for me to reconnect with people the next time we met. Fourteen years later, many of the people from that card database are among my closest friends and clients, and they continue to refer enormous amounts of business to me.

Throughout my selling years, I always treated my career as 'a business within a business'. Although not a proprietary limited company, I spent these years establishing myself as a business entity working within Mercedes-Benz. From the beginning, I set course on a long-term strategy to gain and maintain loyal customers and referrals by understanding and serving people's specific wants and needs. While I was part of a larger sales consultancy team, I focused solely on my ever-growing database of clients, and eventually 100 per cent of my business was coming from repeats and referrals within this network. I personally invested thousands of dollars each year creating and managing a personalised VIP customer club for these clients. This is how I became known as an intrapreneur within the global Mercedes-Benz organisation.

This intrapreneurial business model was drawn to the attention of Mercedes-Benz, where sales staff are encouraged to treat everything they do as if it were their own business — to tear up the list of excuses and take personal responsibility for their actions, acting with integrity and candour in everything they do and keeping the company's best interests at the forefront of their thinking.

EMPLOYEE VS ENTREPRENEUR VS INTRAPRENEUR

In business today, there are three options for staff in organisations:

- Do you want to be an employee, going along in your day-to-day life, content with the security of having a job and not really wanting to rock the boat along the way? Many people are happy to fit into this mould of employee.

- Would you prefer to not have to answer to anyone but yourself? Do you have the courage to go out on your own and to take the risk of starting a new business? These people are the world's entrepreneurs.

- Do you strive for something in between – not content to be an employee, but not prepared for entrepreneurship? Are you courageous, prepared to be a moderate risk-taker, flexible, creative and determined to get results within the construct of an existing organisation? This is the path of the intrapreneur.

Sometimes, employees are given the opportunity to transform their roles into intrapreneurial ones. If you are offered such an opportunity you may have the chance to take your career to new heights by helping to drive the future of your company. Whether you are asked to develop a product, service, channel or application, will you make your mark or seal your fate? Should you:

A. Seize the moment?

B. Pass on the opportunity and remain an employee, or leave to become an entrepreneur?

When to seize the moment – you should go for it when:

- Other employees do not feel empowered to make the needed changes, but you do.

- Other employees do not connect the quality or quantity of their work to the success of your company or an increase in their pay, but you do.

- No one in your company, including your sales team, has ever really had to sell an idea, product or service in order to make a mortgage payment, but you have.

- You see your organisation as just 'going along to get along', but you can't.

When to pass on the opportunity – you should pass and perhaps leave to become an entrepreneur when:

- Your owners are motivated more by protecting their wealth than they are by creating new value for internal and external customers.
- Your owners are threatened, weak and don't really want to change.
- There are insiders protecting the status quo that control your organisation.
- The pain of your organisation changing is greater than the pain of it not changing.

Every effective worker has intrapreneurial traits that may or may not culminate in an entrepreneurial life. Ask yourself how close you are to becoming an entrepreneur. Your answer will help you to decide whether you should seize the moment or pass on the opportunity!

INTRAPRENEURS LEAD NEW BUSINESS GROWTH

When a company is under pressure to grow, organisations of all types look to their roots and their previous successes for answers. Rekindling business growth is often the toughest challenge for a maturing organisation. Can it regain its entrepreneurial spirit and continue to thrive despite its mature culture? By turning to intrapreneurs, the company hopes it can have the best of both worlds.

So how does a company engage intrapreneurs? First, they need to be identified and acknowledged for their unique skill set. Provide them with an appropriate reward and recognition process, embrace their differences and develop the business culture to acknowledge those staff that are intrapreneurs. Challenge them, give them innovative and new business directions that need to be explored and managed as opportunities for the business. The secret is to give them freedom with appropriate responsibility and accountability to the business.

SUCCEEDING AT INTRAPRANEURSHIP – THE TEN COMMANDMENTS

Every new idea will have more than its fair share of detractors, and there is no doubt that being an intrapreneur presents its own difficulties, even in the most tolerant of companies. But by following these Ten Commandments, intrapreneurs can succeed:

1. Do anything to move your idea forward – do any job needed to make your dream work, regardless of your job description.
2. Remember it is easier to ask for forgiveness than for permission.
3. Keep the best interests of the company and its customers in mind, especially when you have to bend the rules or circumvent the bureaucracy.
4. Ask for advice before you ask for resources.
5. Build your team; intrapreneurship is not a solo activity.
6. Share credit widely with your team and the company.
7. Come to work each day willing to be challenged and have the courage to do what's right, rather than what you know.
8. Work underground for as long as you can. Find ways to hide the right new ideas from the corporate immune system in order to keep them alive. Too often the best ideas are prematurely exposed.
9. Be true to your goals, but be realistic about how to achieve them.
10. Honour and educate your sponsors. To keep the project alive, seek out managers whose advice you truly value, show them a 'can-do' creativity and the ability to follow through.

WHAT CAN SENIOR MANAGERS DO?

Let's assume that you want to create an innovative, fast-moving organisation that takes the world by storm. You want process innovation, new products and services, continuous improvements and breakthroughs, new ways to sell old products and services, and to be stronger than your competitors. Your company can achieve these things by finding a way to direct and release the intrapreneurial spirit buried within your employees. Here are some simple steps that will open the doors for innovation and increase the level of discomfort with the status quo:

Adopt a customer: Spend time with your customers and talk to your suppliers. Create a vision or strategic intent that will engage and inspire your employees. It is difficult to give employees the freedom they need to be innovative without engaging them in an inspiring vision.

Create a vision that stretches your organisation beyond 'business as usual': A strategic intent that reaches beyond what seems possible with existing resources requires innovation and transformation, not just incremental improvements. It creates new freedoms and new responsibilities because it requires the creative energy of all employees.

Ask for help: Effective leaders admit that they don't know it all, but they do know that they need the help and creativity of everyone in the organisation to discover new opportunities.

Discover what is blocking innovation and handle it decisively: Create an environment in which people at all levels can get on with the work of turning the vision into a reality. Promote only those who sponsor, rather than block, innovation.

Search for and reward sponsors: Sponsors are the critical link between top-line management and the innovators within the organisation. They select, nurture, guide, fund, educate, question and redirect innovators.

State the type of innovation you want in your organisation: And don't change your mind before these breakthrough projects come to fruition! We have all witnessed many tragedies of interrupted innovation. Keep the system open to all kinds of innovation at all times – continual improvement, process breakthroughs, line extensions, new products and services, new ways of working together, new internal services and new organisational patterns.

Flexibility and choice: The essence of an innovative organisation is flexibility. To be able to build flexible systems that adapt to the challenges at hand, build choice into the lives of your employees. Allow them to exercise their freedom of choice – to spend 15 per cent of their time working on new ideas of their own choosing, and give them more choice over which projects they work on.

Build community: Building community spirit by creating visions of the future for the organisation will address people's deepest values. Make the organisation stand for something that employees can be proud of – something that makes it worthwhile for them to rise above their self-interest and cheer for the whole.

> Innovation begins with an attitude and a willingness to embrace the unknown; factors that are often difficult for an established business to reconcile.

INNOVATION AND INTRAPRENEURSHIP IN ACTION

Innovation begins with an attitude and a willingness to embrace the unknown; factors that are often difficult for an established business to reconcile. But when a company embraces innovation and evolves its traditional approaches, new channels of business that deliver new financial and business development opportunities happen. Mercedes-Benz is an example of one of the 'oldest' modern corporations in the world. It is recognised for its distinct brand and all that it stands for: embracing innovation and change, leading the world in technology, and extraordinary achievements. In staff development, change is being led by individuals who see the future of the business and who are implementing innovative management styles to engage and retain staff, and their successful innovations are then being taught to the rest of the business. An innovation culture has certainly been created within the company, across all areas of the business, including the business models, relationships and methods of using resources. The most recent example of this innovation in action is the new concept dealership, Mercedes-Benz Airport Express.

In February 2006, I accepted the opportunity to manage this exciting new initiative from Mercedes-Benz, it is a dealership concept that has not been seen anywhere in the world before. This innovation was first introduced by a fellow Mercedes-Benz staff member who raised the idea of having a unique Mercedes presence at major Australian airports, and over time our team has expanded on that idea to create an entire service and customer care centre concept. For a few thousand dollars, no more than the cost of a billboard, we could rent some extra space and create an entire terminal where time-poor customers could drop off their Mercedes-Benz for servicing while they are away, and use the Mercedes-Benz valet service to get to and from the domestic or international terminal of their choice. After brainstorming and researching the concept, we found that many luxury car owners are travelling more often, and the time was right for such a concept, so Mercedes-Benz Australia decided to give it a try.

Being presented with the opportunity to manage this exciting new dealership has allowed me to draw on my industry experience gained over the last 14 years. It has allowed the company to take a strategic approach to developing and implementing this concept using innovation and team members' intrapraneurial flair to create a unique, boutique-style dealership which is setting new benchmarks and rewriting the rules for customer service excellence. We now have a business with a new car showroom which comes complete with valet transport to and from the international and domestic airport terminals, dry-cleaning drop off and collection, a gift store with quirky last-minute gifts, relaxation lounge, flight arrival/departure screens and several service bays to service and detail customers' Mercedes-Benz while they are away. The managing director of Mercedes-Benz Australia says, "This is a good example of having an open and creative culture, where it is encouraged and rewarded to speak your mind...what's more, it's managed by the very staff member who originated many of the services offered by this concept".

Peter Baines

PETER BAINES As a detective inspector with the Forensic Services Group of the NSW Police, Peter Baines has led teams in the investigation of some of the world's most horrendous crimes and disasters, including the Bali bombings, the Waterfall train disaster and the Boxing Day tsunami. He is one of Australia's most experienced disaster management specialists. Today, Peter teaches people how to apply the invaluable lessons he has learnt about crisis management to everyday business and life situations. He understands better than most people that during times of extreme crisis, it is focusing on results, not excuses, that will get the job done.

Peter has completed university studies in forensic science, law and management and is the co-founder of Hands Across the Water, a charity that is raising funds to build an orphanage in Thailand. He has touched the lives of many through his work, and continues to do so through his compelling keynote presentations, which take his audiences from laughter to tears as he tells his story and shares the lessons learnt from managing crisis on the world stage.

Lis Brandson

LIS BRANDSON'S passion is investing in people. With a background in research, education, training and communications, Lis broke records in recruitment and business growth with the launch of a major international network marketing company in the late 1990s. Lis is the CEO of Sea Acres Eco-Sanctuary Pty Ltd – a $50 million Eco development on the New South Wales south coast. Lis is recognised as a motivator and personal development mentor. Her motivational, personal growth and wealth psychology seminars have been described as life-changing events.

Lis has a master's degree in international relations, and is the mother of four young children.

Matt Church

MATT CHURCH is one of Australia's foremost experts on personal leadership. His best-selling books *Adrenalin Junkies, Serotonin Seekers* and *Highlife 24/7* have led him to become one of Australia's top 10 conference speakers. When he is not presenting at corporate events he is guiding some of the world's leading thinkers as CEO of the management company, Thought Leaders Limited, the publisher of this book.

As one of the most creative educators in the country, Matt is obsessed with the idea of how the best get better, and he brings this focus to everything he does, whether he is helping high-performance teams or coaching CEOs on strategic communications.

With an academic background in science, Matt likes to prepare messages that are content-rich and pragmatic in their application. He is a past recipient of the coveted Nevin Award, Australia's most prestigious peer acknowledgement for excellence and service to the speaking industry.

Iven Frangi

IVEN FRANGI is Australasia's customer experience management specialist. His career has been built on a foundation of high-level success in sales, sales management and marketing. Before beginning his own company, Iven was the marketing communications manager for the world-leaders in one-to-one marketing, the Peppers + Rogers group. Together with futurist Craig Rispin, Iven co-authored *High Tech – High Touch Selling*, and was a contributor to Allan Pease's best-selling *Body Language*. Iven has been featured on the Business Skills pay-per-view education network and has presented sales and marketing subjects for Deakin University's distance learning program.

Today, Iven's clients include top 100 businesses, franchises, international organisations, major financial services firms and SMEs. His core message is that every interaction with a business is an experience, and his goal is to create bottom-line results for his clients by helping them to 'create experiences their customers can't get anywhere else'.

GISÈLE GAMBI is founder and co-director of Dare to be Remarkable. She works with individuals, leaders and businesses to help them connect with their vision, and to ignite potential and possibility in their lives. Having worked in human resource management in the corporate world, Gisèle saw huge potential to introduce a new technology that would improve how businesses get results, with less effort, less angst and much more joy.

Gisèle has a bachelor of arts, postgraduate diploma in human resource management, certificate in counselling, is accredited in various psychological and behavioural instruments and has completed a three-year intuition and creating program.

DR ADRIAN GEERING has been a mentor, teacher and adviser to CEOs and leaders of high-performing companies and organisations, both individually and in groups, for 20 years. In 2003, Adrian was recognised internationally by TEC International (the leading CEO mentoring and coaching organisation operating in 15 countries with over 11,000 CEO members) with the Donald Cope Award for the best chairman and mentor in the world. He is TEC's longest-serving chairman and regional chairman in Australia. He has earned seven degrees/diplomas, including a PhD in management and adult learning, and is the author of two books.

Adrian's passion is helping leaders and CEOs to leverage their lives, leadership, business and community 100x through high-impact mentoring, teaching and advising. He achieves this through keynote addresses, seminars, writing, facilitating and mentoring both in Australia and overseas. He is currently completing his third book on lessons from the lives of CEOs.

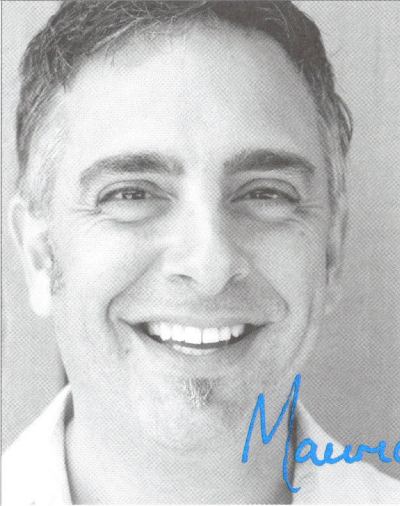

Maurice Goldberg

MAURICE GOLDBERG believes that abundance is achieved when people fuse wealth creation with an understanding of what they love to do. In just over a decade, Maurice has built the Ark Group into one of the fastest-growing wealth and prosperity businesses in Australia. It comprises five companies, has more than $750 million in assets under advisement, and for the past two years *Business Review Weekly* has listed it among Australia's 100 fastest growing businesses.

Maurice is an opinion leader who is regularly quoted by financial broadsheets and business media because of his innovative and non-traditional approach to creating wealth and abundance for both individuals and businesses. He has an honours degree in architecture, a diploma in financial planning, is a certified financial planner, and holds real estate licences around Australia. Maurice is passionate about taking both businesses and people beyond what they thought possible.

Chris Gray

CHRIS GRAY teaches people how to get more from less. Whether you are short of time, money or both, there is always a way to use your situation to your advantage. It just takes a certain mind-set and the ability to leverage everything at your disposal.

Through his company, Red, Chris runs programs to educate teenagers about how they can get an early start on their financial goals, and how that can benefit them in their late twenties and thirties. He facilitates workshops to teach property buyers and investors how they can afford more property while taking less risk. And he is a mentor to CEOs, showing them how to turn their high incomes into passively growing wealth.

Having retired from full-time work himself at the age of 31, Chris is an inspiration to those that hear him speak as he simplifies complicated financial concepts and breaks down financial decisions into factual and unemotional equations.

AVRIL HENRY migrated to Australia in 1980 with two suitcases, $500 and a dream of living freely and making a difference. Her career has spanned senior roles in finance, IT, project management, change management and HR. She has worked for multinational companies in South Africa, Australia, the UK and the USA.

Today, she runs her own business, focusing on public speaking and consulting in leadership, people and performance strategies, and is also an executive coach. Avril seeks to help organisations develop people leadership capability and to create positive, productive work environments. Her clients include the Department of Defence, IBM, CBA, Astra Zeneca, St George Hospital, NSW Health and many others. She recently led a Ministerial Review into recruitment and retention practices in the Australian Army, Navy and Air Force, having been appointed by the Minister of Defence.

Avril is the author of *Leadership Revelations: An Australian Perspective* and *The Who, What, When and Y of Generation whY?*, and has a regular column in *MyBusiness* and *Wealth Creator* magazines.

SHANE KEMPTON Six foot-four and 110kg of pure Western Australian real estate passion, Shane Kempton, alias 'The Commando', began his real estate career in 1991. After three years, he left to pursue a military career with the elite SASR (Special Air Service Regiment), which he served with for five years. After leaving the service, he returned to real estate with the goal of becoming the owner of the number one office by applying the values of loyalty, discipline, humour and camaraderie. Shane not only realised his goal but was appointed CEO of the Roy Weston Group in March 2006.

Shane's meteoric journey has taught him life lessons that he generously passes along as a highly sought-after public speaker, life coach and mentor to people across Australia. The Commando's message is to help people transform from being Worriers to becoming Warriors in life. He teaches self-management principles, along with the basic rules of choice and personal values.

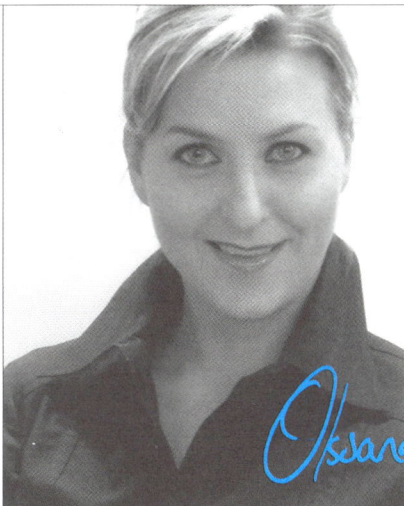

Oksana Koriakova

OKSANA KORIAKOVA Dynamic and always well-presented, Russian-born Australian Oksana Koriakova is the founding director of Impero Group Pty Ltd. She and her team help corporations to identify and utilise their brand equity through targeted promotional products.

As an identity management expert, Oksana believes that everyone has the ability to let their individuality shine; that leadership is the mark of an individual; and that great leaders can only be truly effective when their inner identity is congruent with their outer perception. Her Identity Management program delivers perception analyses and strategies designed to help you enhance your success through your personal brand. If you are looking to be the best leader you can be, and want to see whether your unique identity and values are consistently communicated, then Identity Management is for you.

Helen Macdonald

HELEN MACDONALD is passionate about accessing all areas of businesses and teams to maximise results. She specialises in breaking down the barriers and silos that limit the potential of workplaces, connecting departments and people in powerful ways that create change-ready, highly-functioning, positive environments that increase employee and customer satisfaction, and boost business success.

Helen has worked with companies large and small around the Asia Pacific region, including General Motors, NCR, Hyundai, Ericsson, Hewlett Packard and Tupperware. Her dynamic and highly interactive style encourages her audiences to get involved, take action, and create better outcomes for themselves and their businesses.

Her message is that 'life is too short to live in a box' and she can show you how to create a workplace where customers smile, employees thrive, and productivity and effectiveness reach new heights.

Rick Otton

RICK OTTON is the director of the We Buy Houses Group of Companies that operates in the USA, Australia, New Zealand and the United Kingdom. He is an internationally recognised property expert and speaker on vendor financing.

In 1991, Rick and his American wife, Jane, began buying foreclosed real estate in the USA, and in 2000, tailored their USA system to the Australian marketplace. Today, Rick trains people in his specialised property techniques. His mission is to change the way real estate is transacted around the world. He was recently featured on the ABC TV documentary series, *Reality Bites*.

Lorna Patten

LORNA PATTEN is an expert in helping people create fundamental shifts in relationships. She rigorously questions the way things are and challenges you to think differently about what's really going on. Lorna's thought-provoking and insightful responses to the myriad issues facing people today are based on a very simple philosophy: each of us is always creating the whole of our own reality and who we really are is powerful beyond measure.

In 1999, after 15 years running her own counselling, corporate coaching and training business, Lorna decided to take her exciting personal development work to a wider audience. She created Open Up Communication, a business that offers a powerful, effective, personal development process for the small business market helping leaders, management teams, teams and individuals that desire to change, grow and reach their full potential. But be warned: when you engage Lorna, she will confront you with breathtaking truths and take you to places in your mind, heart and soul that truly are life changing.

Gihan Perera

GIHAN PERERA is an expert in leveraging expertise for profit. He works with speakers, trainers, consultants, coaches, facilitators and other thought leaders, analysing what they are already doing and identifying ways that they can create additional income with minimal effort. His practical strategies create measurable results.

Gihan has been using the internet since before most people even knew it existed. He is the CEO of First Step Communications, an Australian web design company that helps clients around the world to leverage their online strategy to reach new markets, create new products and accelerate their growth.

Sharonne Phillips

SHARONNE PHILLIPS believes in the power of systems. As the developer of The Systems Model™, Sharonne assists individuals and organisations in exposing how their existing systems are serving their best interests or undermining their core purpose. Sharonne has an extraordinary aptitude for discovering the weak links within organisations and implementing systematic change. Change is good; understanding when it is necessary and how to implement it is better!

Sharonne has worked within the health, hospitality, administrative, manufacturing and mining industries for over 25 years, and has worked closely with staff and managers to achieve greater understanding of the relationships between people, processes and systems in diverse situations.

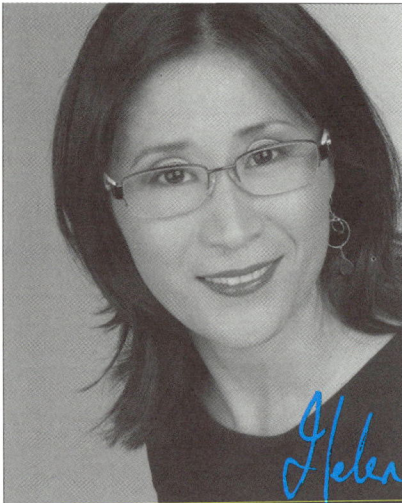

HELEN SHAO was born and raised in the Chinese city of Tianjin during the Cultural Revolution. She has a bachelor of pure mathematics and was a lecturer in mathematics at Tianjin TV University for three years before undertaking a master's in applied mathematics and going on to lecture at the University of Tianjin in economics and finance. Helen came to Australia in 1989 and undertook PhD studies in applied finance.

Helen's interest in managing personal finances grew from her early experiences as a newcomer to Australia, when she needed to adapt herself to the Australian way of transacting, managing and more importantly, saving her money.

Today Helen continues to be passionate about the financial wellbeing of people, working as a financial planner with Fiducian Financial Services in Sydney and a mortgage broker through National Brokers Group. She also runs her own business, the Financial Fitness Class and is the director of the 'Money Magnet Club', providing workshops and other programs on building healthy financial lifestyles to her clients.

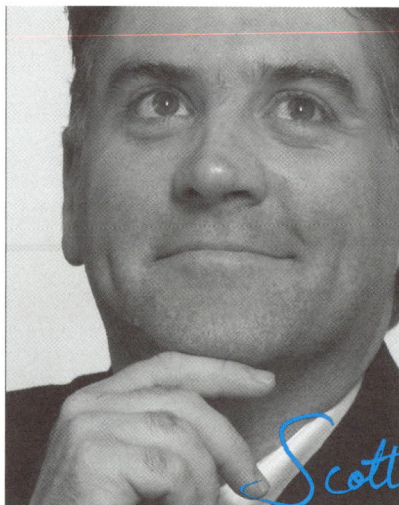

SCOTT STEIN For the past 20 years, Scott has watched as people at home and at work switch off and become numb. As an educator, trainer and coach he has been in a unique position to inspire and challenge many senior executives, as well as their frontline staff, to change the way they think and operate. In his landmark program, Numb™, he teaches individuals and organisations how to improve their performance and get more out of life rather than staying on autopilot. He believes in the philosophy that no matter what happens around you, your life is full of choices.

Scott moved to Sydney, Australia, from the USA over 10 years ago to escape the corporate rat-race but quickly realised that the pace of business and the threat of becoming numb exists in all walks of life. In addition to working with many successful businesses in Australia and overseas, Scott runs three successful businesses of his own, and together with his wife is raising three young children – so he also understands first-hand the dangerous temptation of becoming numb!

Deborah Vanderhoek

DEBORAH VANDERHOEK From full-time mother of three to becoming one of Australia's leading real estate agents, Deborah's is an amazing success story. After 10 years of earning prestigious awards and regularly being the leading female agent in a network of 7,000 agents in the LJ Hooker network, Deborah wrote her first book, *Open for Inspection: Inside the Minds of Australia's Leading Real Estate Agents*. The book went on to sell over 2,500 copies and is now used as a training manual in many real estate organisations.

Deborah has been a keynote speaker at many international conferences and she combines her unique blend of business and heart in all her endeavours. Today Deborah continues to run one of Sydney's leading real estate offices, LJ Hooker Bondi Junction, with her husband and spends whatever spare time she has writing her first novel, travelling to exotic destinations, being with her family and using her blend of enthusiasm and energy on charity projects.

Nils Vesk

NILS VESK is an expert on the process of coming up with and executing great ideas. As a professional designer, Nils has applied his skills in creativity execution for many of Australia's leading companies.

With a 'creating' mind-set Nils has worked internationally as a designer in a wide range of challenging situations from designing new cities in Indonesia and prisons in Australia, to hosting and designing television fitness programs. Most recently, Nils has been consulting and transforming companies' creative execution. Nils is continually speaking and facilitating to thousands of people through his powerful and entertaining keynotes and workshops.

Nils has completed university studies in design in both the USA and Australia and is the author of the best-selling book, *Life's Little Toolbox*. His latest book takes people through the 'Create' process for coming up with good ideas and transforming them into reality.

Mark Wayland

MARK WAYLAND has two passions: the first is for learning and development programs to be tied closely to the business's bottom line. That is, for programs to be directly linked to changing behaviours that increase profitability. The second is to enable business owners, managers and their staff to master the art and science of face-to-face communication, especially in managing employees and selling in the 21st century, and in doing so, to produce above-average business results.

His expertise and experience stem from a successful 25-year career in learning and development, sales, management and education.

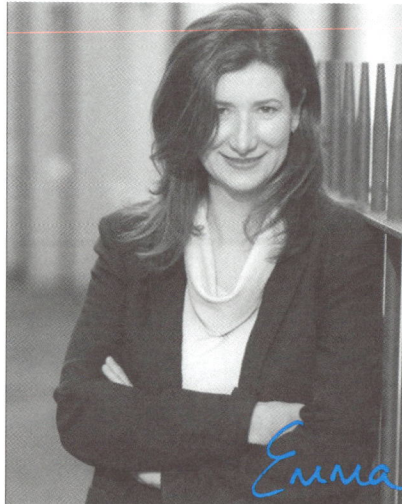

Emma Weber

EMMA WEBER is the managing director of Vivat, a specialist learning company that helps companies maximise their learning opportunities through 'Turning Learning into Action™'.

Emma has personally worked with more than 500 people in a variety of industries who want to better themselves and their learning opportunities. Among her client base are some of Australia's most respected companies.

The Australian Institute of Training and Development (AITD) nominated Vivat as a finalist in the National Awards for Innovation in Learning in 2004. In 2005 Vivat was a finalist as part of the BMW nomination in the national *Human Resources* magazine award for best learning and development strategy.

Emma believes that knowledge is only useful when it is transferred into action and is committed to taking this principle into organisations to support both training programs and conferences.

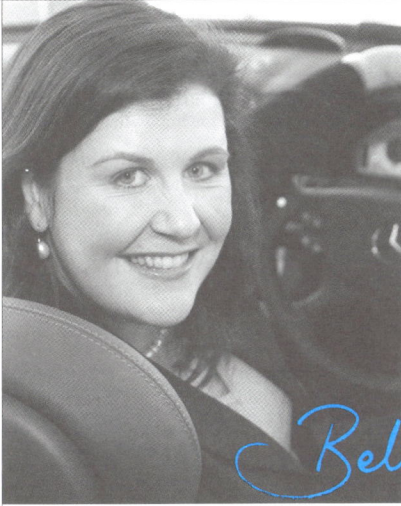

Belinda Yabsley

BELINDA YABSLEY has built a laudable reputation for innovation in the art of customer relationship management. At 31, she is the first female and youngest general manager of a Mercedes-Benz dealership in Australia, launching the innovative Mercedes-Benz Airport Express dealership in February 2006. Belinda achieved this position in recognition of her extraordinary sales records and her ingenuity in creating a business-within-a-business model, within the global organisation of DaimlerChrysler. Known in Australia as 'Miss Mercedes', Belinda achieved much-publicised recognition within the Australian motor industry in 2004, when she sold the first customised luxury Maybach saloon for $1 million.

For Belinda, relationships do not stop after a sale – her customers become her friends. This level of commitment and compassion is evidenced by the fact that 100 per cent of her business comes from repeat and glowing referrals. In 2005, she was honoured as the Sydney Businesswoman of the Year and was named a NSW Finalist in the 2004 and 2005 Telstra Businesswomen's Awards. Belinda is dedicated to sharing and mentoring people from all walks of life on an international and local level. She currently sits on two boards, is an ambassador for several charities and is a mentor for the NSW Premier's Department.

To contact Thought Leaders or any
of the contributors in this book:

VISIT

www.thoughtleaders.com.au